# **About** Island Press

Since 1984, the nonprofit Island Press has been stimulating, shaping, and communicating the ideas that are essential for solving environmental problems worldwide. With more than 800 titles in print and some 40 new releases each year, we are the nation's leading publisher on environmental issues. We identify innovative thinkers and emerging trends in the environmental field. We work with world-renowned experts and authors to develop cross-disciplinary solutions to environmental challenges.

Island Press designs and implements coordinated book publication campaigns in order to communicate our critical messages in print, in person, and online using the latest technologies, programs, and the media. Our goal: to reach targeted audiences—scientists, policymakers, environmental advocates, the media, and concerned citizens—who can and will take action to protect the plants and animals that enrich our world, the ecosystems we need to survive, the water we drink, and the air we breathe.

Island Press gratefully acknowledges the support of its work by the Agua Fund, Inc., Annenberg Foundation, The Christensen Fund, The Nathan Cummings Foundation, The Geraldine R. Dodge Foundation, Doris Duke Charitable Foundation, The Educational Foundation of America, Betsy and Jesse Fink Foundation, The William and Flora Hewlett Foundation, The Kendeda Fund, The Andrew W. Mellon Foundation, The Curtis and Edith Munson Foundation, Oak Foundation, The Overbrook Foundation, the David and Lucile Packard Foundation, The Summit Fund of Washington, Trust for Architectural Easements, Wallace Global Fund, The Winslow Foundation, and other generous donors.

The opinions expressed in this book are those of the author(s) and do not necessarily reflect the views of our donors.

# HUMAN TRANSIT

JARRETT WALKER

# Human Transit

How Clearer Thinking About
Public Transit Can Enrich Our
Communities and Our Lives

*Illustrations by*

Eric Orozco

Erin Walsh

Alfred Twu

Daniel Howard

David Jones

 **ISLAND**PRESS

Washington | Covelo | London

ISLAND PRESS is a trademark of the Center for Resource Economics.


Library of Congress Cataloging-in-Publication Data

Walker, Jarrett, 1962–
    Human transit : how clearer thinking about public transit can enrich our communities and our lives / Jarrett Walker ; Illustrations by Eric Orozco ... [et al.].
        p.   cm.
    Includes bibliographical references and index.
    ISBN-13: 978-1-59726-971-1 (cloth : alk. paper)
    ISBN-10: 1-59726-971-9 (cloth : alk. paper)
    ISBN-13: 978-1-59726-972-8 (pbk. : alk. paper)
    ISBN-10: 1-59726-972-7 (pbk. : alk. paper)  1. Local transit.  2. City planning.
3. Community development.  I. Title.
    HE4211.W27   2011
    388.4—dc23
                                        2011026554


Printed on recycled, acid-free paper

Manufactured in the United States of America
10  9  8  7  6  5  4  3


KEYWORDS: bus, Complete Streets, density, express service, light rail, local service, mapping, mobility, network branding, operating costs, peak commute period, peak-only service, rail, rapid service, subway, transit fare, transit planning, transit policy, transit station, transit stop, urban form

# CONTENTS

# ACKNOWLEDGMENTS

When it comes to cities, conversation and collaboration are the essence of creativity. This book arises out of twenty years of practice as a consultant plus fifteen years as an advocate, so it reflects conversations with many hundreds of engaged and dedicated people. It would be impossible to list everyone whose insights and perspectives influenced this book.

Still, three people are responsible for my being in this field at all. In the 1970s, Bill Allen, then of Portland's transit agency TriMet, found the time and patience to talk with an enthusiastic and detail-obsessed teenager. Tom Matoff, as TriMet's head of planning in 1983, gave me my first planning job and proved by his example that transit can be a humanistic and even aesthetic pursuit. Bonnie Nelson of Nelson\Nygaard gave me the break that restarted my planning career in 1990.

My most recent boss, Neil Cagney, of the Australian consulting firm MRCagney, saw the book's potential and helped push the project along. I'm grateful to all of my colleagues at his firm.

While writing, I spent a crucial month at the Centre for the Public Awareness of Science at the Australian National University, where the faculty and doctoral candidates were generous with feedback and insights; thanks to the Centre's Dr. Will Grant for that opportunity. I'm also grateful for the friendship of Professors David Hensher and Corinne Mulley of the University of Sydney's Institute for Transport and Logistics Studies, and especially their "Thredbo" conference series. I've also found an intellectual home at the planning division of the greater Vancouver transit agency TransLink, which supports creative thought as well as any university.

Friends and colleagues who read the entire first draft include Brian Mills, Dale Favier, Gordon Price, Jack Lattemann, Yonah Freemark, Aaron Renn, and Bill Bryant. All offered helpful comments. I'm also grateful for the feedback of Peter Timms, Peter Schmiedeskamp, Sandy Thomas, Todd Gilens, Anthony Perl, Anthony Mifsud, David Sucher, Duncan Watry, and Jeff Deby. Charlotte-based architect Eric Orozco of Neighboring Concepts PLLC is credited as an illustrator but was also a key source of advice.

For the editing phase, Karl Lindeson and Lindsay Pratt gave me the use of their country home in Berrima, Australia, where the landscape and wild-life were a constant inspiration.

Crucial transit agency perspectives came from Nathan Banks of Portland's TriMet, Conan Cheung of the Los Angeles County Metropolitan Transportation Authority, Doran Barnes of Foothill Transit (east of Los Angeles), and Paul Bignardi of the San Francisco Municipal Transportation Agency. Responsibility for the book's ideas and errors remains with me.

My professional blog, HumanTransit.org, has drawn an international group of regular commenters whose lively discussion has done much to clarify my thinking. I wish I could list the hundred or more people who have contributed substantially to this conversation in blog comments, through email, and in person at various events.

Finally, my editor, Heather Boyer of Island Press, was patient, creative, and resourceful in helping produce this book. I'm grateful to Island Press for seeing the book's potential and helping to create its final shape.

# INTRODUCTION

Suddenly, public transit is a critical issue.

For decades, the private car has seemed the ideal tool for free and spontaneous travel, and in rural areas and many small towns, that will continue to be true. But all over the world, people are moving into cities, and great cities just don't have room for everyone's car. Meanwhile, the converging threats of climate change and the end of cheap oil are forcing a new assessment of how cities work. Public transit—the most efficient means for large numbers of people to move freely within cities—is an essential tool in that effort. Today, even Los Angeles, a city that is world famous for its extreme dependence on cars, is scrambling to grow its transit system as fast as it can manage.[1]

The frustrations of urban transportation have fed a growing public interest in public transit in many countries. But when well-intentioned people look at the public transit around them, many conclude that it does not make sense for them to use it. There are many good reasons not to use transit. It may not go where you need it to go, or at the time you need to go. Perhaps you can get there three times faster by driving, or at half the cost. You may know from experience that you can't trust your service to come on time. Your transit agency's vehicles and staff may fail to meet the most basic standards for civility, safety, and comfort. Your transit network may be too confusing, requiring you to wade through too much detail to figure out whether the service is useful to you.

Even if you decide that you can't use it yourself, you may support transit in hopes that *someone* will use it, because there is obviously not enough

1

room in your city for everyone to drive, or enough space to build more freeways and to widen streets. You may also understand the many kinds of long-term environmental harm associated with too many cars and too much pavement. You may even fear that driving your car while wanting fewer cars in your city is some sort of hypocrisy on your part. (Often it's not. You may live and travel in an area where no reasonably efficient transit can ever provide you with useful service.)

These common frustrations explain why, in many urban regions, support for public transit is wide but shallow. Voters typically support transit in general, but most don't know how to decide whether a transit proposal is good or bad. They may want better transit for themselves or their communities but have no idea how to make it happen.

What is quality public transit? Who can realistically expect to be served by it? What kinds of quality matter? How do we recognize and nurture them? What are the goals we want transit to achieve, and how do we navigate tough spots where these goals conflict?

Debates about transit proposals commonly lose track of these questions. Too often, we defer to a small group of intensely interested people (such as developers, activists, neighborhood groups, labor unions, and purveyors of transit technology) because the debate seems too technical for most of us to follow. As a result, we sometimes end up with transit investments that don't really do what we expected, or that have side effects that should have been foreseen.

Transit debates also suffer from the fact that today, in most of our cities, most of our decision makers are motorists. No matter how much you support transit, driving a car every day can shape your thinking in powerful, subconscious ways. For example, in most debates about proposed rapid transit lines, the *speed* of the proposed service gets more political attention than how *frequently* it runs, even though frequency, which determines waiting time, often matters more than speed in determining how long your trip will take. Your commuter train system will advertise that it can whisk you into the city in 39 minutes, but if the train comes only once every 2 hours and you've just missed one, *your* travel time will be 159 minutes, so it may be faster to drive, or even walk.

I can explain the concept of frequency to a group of well-intentioned motorists, and they may understand why it's important. But what they know is the experience of driving, where speed matters and frequency doesn't. So when they make a decision about a transit project, they are likely to give frequency too little weight. The result can be services that are very fast but don't come when we need them, or that require too much time to connect from one service to another.

The unconscious assumptions of motorists are just one example of how people try to think about transit as though it were something else. Everyone tries to translate a question into terms that they understand. Economists may talk about transit in terms of profitability, as though that were its goal. Social service advocates think of it as a tool for meeting the needs of the disadvantaged. Architects and urban designers care about how it feels to move through a city, so they often focus on the aesthetics of the transit vehicle and infrastructure. Urban redevelopment advocates categorize services according to how well they stimulate development. None of these perspectives is wrong; transit can serve all of these interests and more. But to achieve that broad level of service, these points of view have to be brought together into a clearer conversation.

To aid that conversation, this book aims to give you a grasp of how transit works as an urban mobility tool and how it fits into the larger challenge of urban transportation. This is not a course designed to make you a qualified transit planner, though some professionals will benefit from it. My goal is simply to give you the confidence to form and advocate clear opinions about what kind of transit you want and how that can help create the kind of city you want.

## WHO IS THE PUBLIC? WHO IS AN EXPERT?

When our elected leaders make decisions about transit, they face a noisy mix of competing interests. A senior citizen has trouble walking to a bus stop, so wants the stops placed closer together. Others want the bus stops farther apart, so that the buses run faster. A merchant wants the bus to deviate into his shopping center, to bring customers. Another merchant wants the bus out of his shopping center, because it's bringing "undesirable" people. Suburb A wants a proposed rail transit line to go underground through their community, to preserve their ambience. Farther out on the proposed line, Suburb B wants the whole line elevated, so that the line is cheap enough to get all the way to Suburb B in its first phase.

Transit professionals are not always in a position to clarify the debate. Some of them lack a sufficiently broad view of their product or have been trained to think only about one aspect of it. Many more have the understanding but lack the confidence. Even worse, professionals who work inside transit agencies often find their time consumed by daily crises and controversies and simply don't have time to take a wider view.

For a variety of reasons, transit planning has not evolved as a credentialed discipline—like law, engineering, or architecture—where everyone has to pass a particular course of studies before they can be licensed to work. Transit agencies often value "real-world" experience more than education, but there's no agreement in the industry about which world is real or which experience is useful. In my work as a transit planner, I have met many managers of transit planning who had been hired directly from other fields, with expertise in planning, perhaps, but not in transit. I have met bus drivers who had been transformed into managers, knowing nothing of the craft of management. Some of these people learn fast, adapt, and thrive, but others feel defensive and turn into obstacles.

The openness of the transit planning field—the ease with which it can be entered from related areas—has many advantages. The last thing we need is another closed and revered priesthood enforcing a uniform dogma, like the generation of highway engineers who designed America's interstate system. The principles of transit planning are simple enough that nobody needs a graduate degree to understand them. Anyone who is willing to keep learning should be welcomed into the transit professions.

On the other hand, there really are some facts about how transit works, and they are not all intuitively obvious. In fact, some of them will seem intuitively wrong until you stop to think about them. Most of these facts arise from math, geometry, and occasionally physics, so they're true everywhere, of every technology, and in every culture. If you're going to form intelligent opinions about transit, so that you advocate projects that actually serve your goals, you'll need to understand these basics.

These underlying facts of transit force us to make hard decisions, but they also open up possibilities. My aim is to help you see the unavoidable hard choices and to form your own view on them, but also to help you feel optimistic about the range of things transit can do and how a smart use of transit can improve your community. Like any box of tools, transit can do a lot of useful things, but only if you know each tool's purpose. Much of the noisy confusion in transit debates is the sound of people using a hammer to turn a screw, or a screwdriver to pound nails.

## LISTEN TO YOUR PLUMBER: VALUES VERSUS EXPERTISE

A core idea of this book is that we will have clearer conversations, and make better decisions, if we distinguish carefully between *values* and *expertise* and understand their interplay in our transit debates.

Values are statements about your community's ideals, goals, and priorities. They answer questions like these:

- *What is transit's purpose?* How should we measure the results of our transit system? Ridership? Emissions? Complaints?
- *What counts as adequate and useful transportation?* What, for example, is the minimum level of quality that transit should be aiming for?
- *What kind of city do you want?* Transit, like all transportation infrastructure, can have big impacts on the form, feel, and functioning of your city, so it's important to understand those impacts in advance.

Experts like me can clarify these questions but shouldn't be answering them for you. *My job in this book is not to make you share my values but to give you the tools to clarify and advocate yours.* You, and your community, get to choose "what" you want and "why." An expert's job is to help with "how." It's a crucial distinction, one that often gets lost in transit debates.

But here's the catch: *the expert gets to ask you questions that clarify what you want.* Say you hire a man to fix your plumbing. He goes to work, but soon he encounters a point where he could do one thing or another and it has to be your decision. He says: "I can fix it up for now for $50, and it'll work for a year or so. Or, if I replace the whole whatsit assembly and connect it with a new doohickey, it'll be just like new, but that would be about $700 and it would take a week for the part to get here from Malaysia."

The plumber's question reveals that values ("what") and expertise ("how") have to interact more than once. A transit planner working for your community is like a plumber: he's there to implement your values, not his. But you can't just tell the expert what you want and leave the room. When a leader or manager does this ("Just do it this way—I don't care how you do it!"), he's likely to be unhappy with the results. The values and the expertise must engage in a conversation.

Fortunately, as with plumbing, the questions that transit experts will have about your values are predictable. The same kinds of questions come up over and over. For this reason, the best way to form a resilient and credible opinion about transit is to think carefully about these typical "plumber's questions" and to discuss them within your community. This book is designed to help you do that.

By definition, these questions are hard, because they're about choosing between different things that you like. Your plumber is asking you if you'd like to save money now or have a more permanent fix. "Both" is not a useful answer. A transit expert helping your community has to ask many similar questions. Here are some of the big ones that we'll explore:

- Is transit mostly about serving a peak-period or "rush hour" commute pattern, or is its top priority to provide a consistent service all day? (chapter 6)
- Would you rather have a direct but infrequent service or a more frequent service that requires a connection? (chapter 12)
- Is the goal of your transit system to carry as many people as possible? Or to serve disadvantaged persons who really need the service? Or something else? Or is it a balance of these, and if so, where do you strike that balance? (chapter 10)

These questions arise, unavoidably, from the underlying geometry of transit. This book explores each question in detail. Many people are trying to make transit do things that are geometrically impossible, so it's important to start by exploring how transit works in these terms before going on to the question of technology.

## TECHNOLOGY: TOOL OR GOAL?

When someone asks me what I do, and I say I'm a transit planner, their next question is almost always about technology. They ask my opinion about a rail transit proposal that's currently in the news, or ask me what I think about light rail, or monorails, or jitneys. They assume, like many journalists, that the *choice of technology* is the most important transit planning decision.

Technology choices do matter, but the fundamental geometry of transit is exactly the same for buses, trains, and ferries. If you jump too quickly to the technology choice question but get the geometry wrong, you'll end up with a useless service no matter how attractive its technology is.

What's more, the most basic features that determine whether transit can serve us well are not technology distinctions. Speed and reliability, for example, are mostly about what can get in the way of a transit service. Both buses and rail vehicles can be fast and reliable if they have an exclusive lane or track. Both can also be slow and unreliable if you put them in a congested lane with other traffic. Technology choice, by itself, rarely guarantees a successful service, and many of the most crucial choices are not about technology at all.

## TRANSIT AND URBAN FORM

Many of the "plumber's questions" about transit will be easier or harder because of the way your city is laid out. The physical design of cities determines transit outcomes far more than transit planning does. Your particular location in the city, and the nature of the development and street patterns, will govern the quality of transit you can expect. For that reason, one of the most urgent needs related to transit is to help people make smarter decisions about where to locate their homes and businesses, depending on the level of transit mobility that matters to them.

These decisions, aggregated across the whole population and over many years, can change the shape of your city for better or for worse. Ultimately, our cities grow and change due to individual decisions about where to locate things. It may seem that the developers, planners, and politicians are making these decisions, but all citizens are part of the market that they serve. So everyone contributes to determining whether transit can work in a particular city or development. Chapter 14 is about how to make those choices more wisely.

## WHO AM I? WHO ARE YOU?

Finally, because so little agreement exists about what constitutes expertise in transit, it is only fair that I answer the question: "Who is this guy, and why should I care what he thinks?"

Since 1990, I have been a consultant specializing in transit service design—that is, designing transit networks and their schedules to provide the best possible service to a community, according to the values each community expresses. I've also worked as an in-house consultant in major transit agencies, serving temporarily as part of their staffs. In many cities, from small towns to large urban areas, I can point to places where my service designs are working on the street and have made a clear difference in the relevance of transit. The core pleasure of my professional life is to see transit working well in the real world.

Ever since I was ten years old and began riding the city buses across Portland, Oregon, to school, I have been an attentive customer of transit, constantly musing about how this or that could work better. Phoning the planners at Portland's transit agency, TriMet, I found them interested in talking with me and receptive to new ideas, so I never learned the debilitating cynicism that so many citizens feel—the sense that their transit agencies are so stuck in their ways that there's no point in providing input. Though I sometimes criticize them, I am proud of Portland's city and regional governments, and continue to admire what they are achieving.

Finally, I spent my twenties doing a PhD in a literature field, so I'm extremely sensitive to the workings of language. Throughout the book, I'll point out situations where word choices matter and where the structure of our language may be preventing us from thinking clearly. But enough about me. Who are you?

In writing this book, I imagine that you, the reader, are a curious and thoughtful person who cares about whether we find our way to more rational forms of urban mobility. Perhaps you work or study in a field related to transit, such as land use planning, traffic engineering, or real estate development. You may be a community or business leader, a journalist, or a committed activist. Perhaps you have come to transit issues from another concern, such as the economic development of your city, or the rights of the disabled, or the well-being of seniors, or some form of environmentalism. Perhaps you have used and admired the transit systems of other cities and wonder why those systems aren't possible where you live. Perhaps you are simply a citizen who doesn't like what is happening to your city, who is not sure how to evaluate the transit disputes flaring around you, and who wants to hold more confident opinions. This book is for you if you come to the question of transit with clear ideas about what you want for your city and curiosity about how transit could help you achieve that.

## WHERE ARE YOU?

The core ideas of this book apply anywhere in the world, but my focus is on the United States, Canada, Australia, and New Zealand. These countries share not only affluence by world standards but also an important feeling of spaciousness that comes from having a lot of land and only a few centuries of urban history. For that reason, these countries have led the world in building low-density, car-dependent cities—the hardest and most interesting challenge for public transit. Still, readers in other developed countries will find most of the book useful as well.

As for the less affluent or "developing" world, the geometry is the same but one crucial aspect is different. The cost of running transit in wealthy countries is usually dominated by the cost of labor—drivers, mechanics, and so on. In the developing world, labor is much cheaper, and fewer people own cars, so transit is cheaper to operate and has a larger customer base. That means transit is often a profitable small business—as small as one driver and his bus—and, therefore, is often abundant but poorly organized. Cheaper labor also means that smaller vehicles are economical, so developing world cities tend to have a diverse range of minibuses, shared taxis, and the like.

Although transit's costs and markets differ in the developing world, the same limitations of urban space do apply. Often, the abundance of minibuses and shared taxis is enough to create near gridlock even without many private cars. Today, the developing world is the site of frenetic development of modern bus systems, bus rapid transit, and sometimes rail transit. As these countries grow more prosperous, they face many of the same issues that we in the wealthier countries face now, so I hope readers in the developing world will find the book useful as well.

## WHO ARE "WE"? WHO DECIDES?

Throughout this book, I use "we" to mean you and your fellow citizens in a democratically governed city, along with me as your hired transit planning expert. I assume, in short, that as a citizen, you're someone whose opinion matters, and that if you get together with your fellow citizens and think together with the benefit of an expert's advice, you can arrive at your own resilient view of what you want transit to do—and thus of what kind of transit you need.

If you've spent any time following transit politics in a big urban area, this notion may seem naive. Perhaps you've dealt with cities where a tangle of government agencies works on transit, often quarrelling more than they cooperate. Perhaps you've dealt with bureaucracies that seem defensive, trapped by their own fears and habits, and unwilling to engage you in respectful conversation.

Perhaps, too, you suspect that a small, self-interested elite really makes all the decisions that matter, and that public consultation is just a show. If so, you're probably wrong about that. In twenty years in this business, I've seen plenty of frustrating, confused, and hijacked decision processes. If I wanted to be bitter and cynical, I would have the experience to justify it. But I've seen another pattern: the involvement of more informed and caring citizens—expressing themselves with courtesy, clarity, and persistence— almost always leads to better outcomes.

In any debate, there will be people at the decision table who care only about their personal interests and needs. If those people have the decision table to themselves, you'll get decisions that serve those interests but may not serve your city.

But in situations where lots of citizens care, and choose to learn a bit about transit so that they can advocate more clearly and confidently, better decisions get made, decisions that lead to better mobility, a stronger economy, a more just society, or whatever goal the community is pursuing. *Political leaders make good decisions when informed and caring citizens want them to.* It's only when they sense that citizens have given up or don't care that they may let narrower interests carry the day. I see this pattern over and over.

So if you're willing to learn a bit about how transit works, what it does well, what it doesn't do, and how it fits into the larger challenge of the city, your opinion will count.

## RESPECT FOR TRANSIT

Throughout this book, you'll be asked to develop a respect for transit not just as a tool but also as an area of expertise. Many people look at transit lines running back and forth in their city and feel that it *looks easy*. Many other people think they understand transit because they understand something that's connected to it, such as urban design, operations management, economics, or traffic engineering. Get all those people in a room and they start arguing and talking past one another, often hurling jargon as a weapon. Other citizens listen to a bit of this and decide that transit is impossible to figure out.

It's actually not hard to understand transit and how it can serve our values and needs, if we approach it with some respect. Let's try.

### Continue the Conversation

As you read this book, you'll have questions. You are welcome to submit these at http://www.humantransit.org, using the email button under my photo. I will post replies to frequently asked questions, including links to further sources, at http://www.humantransit.org/faq. Please join me in continuing the conversation.

# 1

# WHAT TRANSIT IS AND DOES

There are several ways to define public transit,[a] so it is important to clarify how I'll be using the term. Public transit *consists of regularly scheduled vehicle trips, open to all paying passengers, with the capacity to carry multiple passengers whose trips may have different origins, destinations, and purposes.*

Let's take this definition apart:

- *"regularly scheduled vehicle trips"*: Transit is provided by a vehicle running on a regular schedule or pattern. There is room for variation in routes and schedules. Demand-responsive services, for example, may vary their routing according to customer requests, within set limits. But at its core, transit service must be predictable so that different people can plan around it without coordinating directly with one another. This feature is the crucial difference between transit and other ways of sharing a ride.
- *"open to all paying passengers"*: The word *public* in *public transit* means "open to the entire public." This word can be confusing in debates about whether transit should be operated by the government or by the private sector. In the developed world, where wage costs are high, transit is usually subsidized by government, but it may still be operated either by government or by private companies. In those conversations, *public transit* can be misunderstood as meaning "transit operated by the public sector—that is, government—rather than by private

---

[a] In Great Britain and most other Commonwealth countries outside North America, the term is not "public transit" but "public transport." My definition would be the same.

companies." That is *not* the meaning in this book or the prevalent meaning in the developed world. Even privately operated transport services are expected to welcome all paying customers; in fact, the failure to do so can become a civil rights issue.[b]

- *"that can carry multiple passengers"*: The ability to carry many people with a single vehicle is the defining virtue of transit, and the most basic measure of its efficiency.
- *"whose trips may have different origins, destinations, and purposes"*: Transit, in the sense used in this book, does not include:
  - carpools and vanpools, where several people with the same destination share a ride;
  - school buses, where school is the only origin or destination served;
  - a family in their minivan, or any other group that's intentionally traveling together;
  - taxis, which carry a small number of riders at the time, typically all with the same origin and destination.[c]

There are many forms of multi-occupant vehicles, all of which are better for the environment than the same individuals each driving alone. Carpools, school buses, and shared taxis are all useful parts of a city's transportation mix, and sometimes demand can be shifted between these services and the formal public transit system. But they are not *public transit* as this book, and most of the industry, uses the term.

At its core, transit is about multiple people riding in one vehicle even though they are not intentionally traveling together or even going to the same places. The core challenge of transit design, then, is how to run vehicles so that people with different origins, destinations, and purposes can

---

[b] A service open only to a subset of the public—such as paratransit vans that serve disabled persons on demand—can count as public transit if it specifically serves persons who cannot access regular transit services. The spirit of paratransit is to serve people who cannot use regular transit service for reasons of disability, so even though it's closed to other riders, it still serves the goal of a total service offering that is available to everyone. The US Americans with Disabilities Act, for example, requires paratransit service to exist only when and where fixed route services for the general public exist.

[c] Taxis are sometimes used as transit vehicles at low-demand times, and in these cases they satisfy the definition of transit that I'm using here. However, taxis hired for the *exclusive* use of one person or party—the usual taxi model in the developed world—are outside of this definition of transit.

make their trip at the same time and will be motivated to choose transit to do so. This book is all about that challenge.

## TRANSIT'S ROLE IN A COLLABORATION OF MODES

While this book is about transit, I never imply that transit is or should be the dominant alternative to the private car. Many ways of sharing vehicles have important roles to play in the larger project of reducing car dependence. These include many forms of carpooling and vanpooling, which typically carry people from a similar area of origin to a common destination, as well as "carshare" programs, which provide members with hourly self-service car rental, thus reducing a household's need to own cars. These programs, commonly supported by transit agencies,[d] are important complements to transit, though they are not this book's focus.

In focusing on transit, I am also not denying the role of the "active modes," such as cycling and walking. Quite the opposite. Virtually every transit rider is also a pedestrian, so transit ridership depends heavily on the quality of the pedestrian environment where transit stops.[e] The ability and willingness of people to walk a short distance to a stop or station is what makes it possible to gather many people with many intentions on a single vehicle, which is the essence of transit's project.

Cycling, meanwhile, is growing rapidly in many New World cities, at least those that have made some effort to accommodate it. But even in the most bicycle-dominated countries, such as the Netherlands, transit has a crucial market. Local bus service has a somewhat smaller role there because bicycles take so much of the short-distance market, but in the longer-distance market, trips over 3 miles (5 km)[f] or so, cycling and transit reinforce each

---

[d] "Agency" is a common North American word for the organization running public transit, so I'll use it in this book. Your city's term may differ, as there are many ways public transit can be organized within government.

[e] Throughout this book, I will have to ask some disabled persons and their advocates to forgive my use of the terms *walking* and *pedestrian*. These terms are sometimes considered objectionable because a person in a wheelchair is technically not walking or traveling by foot. My use of these terms explicitly *includes* persons in wheelchairs and similar devices that allow them to travel at typical pedestrian speeds.

[f] Throughout this book, "km" preceded by a number means kilometers, while "m" means meters.

other. Longer-distance "rapid transit" services (rail and bus) run fast by not stopping often, but their stations feature masses of bicycle parking. The bicycle becomes an ideal tool for extending the reach of a rapid transit station, reducing (but not eliminating) the need for slower local bus and streetcar services.

Many cities and transit agencies are looking at how to expand the potential for these "cycle + transit" trips. These efforts include enhancing bicycle storage opportunities at stations as well as allowing cyclists to bring their bikes onboard, at least during low-demand times when there's room to spare. These strategies have the potential to build the market for both cycling and public transit.

So transit has the potential for a mutually beneficial relationship with most of the other alternatives to the private car.

- *Walking* is an intrinsic feature of almost all transit trips, so all transit advocates must be pedestrian advocates. Transit outcomes depend heavily on the nature of the walking required, including both how long the walk is and how pleasant it is.
- *Cycling* can compete with local transit but tends to complement longer-distance rapid transit, especially when investments are made in secure bicycle storage at stations.
- *Carpooling* is a crucial tool for regularly scheduled commutes, especially to lower-density employment centers, such as business and industrial parks, that are not dense enough to attract high-quality transit.
- *Carsharing,* a form of short-term car rental, is essential in cities that want to encourage lower levels of car ownership, at least in their denser neighborhoods where the space requirements of private cars are hardest to meet. Carsharing eliminates the temptation to own a car that you only need once or twice a week, by providing the cheaper option of shared cars for these purposes.

So even as these other sustainable transport modes grow, we will need public transit. Among the sustainable transportation alternatives, public transit is unique in two crucial respects. First, only public transit can carry large numbers of people in a single vehicle with a single driver,[g] even as

---

[g] Most public transit vehicles have one on-board employee, whom I'll colloquially call the driver. Many US transit agencies prefer the word *operator*, but that word would sound

these people travel from different origins to different destinations for different purposes. At the intense levels of demand found in high-density cities, public transit is an efficient use of both energy and scarce urban space and is often the most attractive option for trips that are too long to walk or cycle.

Second, public transit delivers people from one part of the city to another *as pedestrians*, eliminating all the challenges of storing a personal vehicle. The pedestrian is the foundation of contemporary urban design, because walking is the only form of transportation that doesn't feel like transportation at all. Walking is also an ideal mode for both health and sustainability. If you want to encourage pedestrian life, you need to connect pedestrian-intensive places to one another in a way that the pedestrian can use. Transit can be ideal for this purpose.

## FIXED OR FLEXIBLE?

To make a vehicle trip useful to many people who are not coordinating with one another, the vehicle trip has to be predictable. That's why, in the developed world, transit is dominated by *fixed* services; on these, transit vehicles follow the same path, at the same time, day after day, so that customers can plan around the pattern. Fixed services are the most efficient form of transit in terms of the ability to carry many passengers for each hour of the driver's time, so they have come to represent well over 99 percent of transit ridership in the United States.

The rest, accounting for less than 1 percent of ridership, are various kinds of flexible or demand-responsive services, where the routing followed by a transit bus or van can change based on customer requests. Although flexible route services are an area of great innovation, they remain limited because they're intrinsically less efficient. Taking a different route depending on customer requests, as flexible routes do, takes more of the driver's time for each passenger's needs. So flexible routes tend to be useful where the overall demand is low, or for specific populations whose needs aren't met by fixed services, such as some disabled persons. I'll return to

---

too vague in a book for the general reader. Note, however, that a driver's job varies considerably from one service to another, and in some cases, such as certain rapid transit trains, they aren't really driving at all.

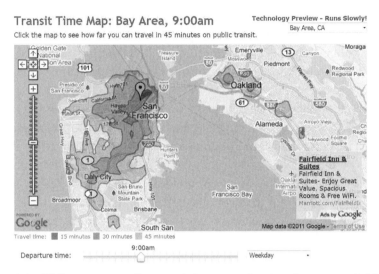

**Figure 1-1** Walkscore.com online travel time map showing the area reachable by transit from a user-specified location in a user-specified period of time. Bands represent 15-minute intervals. *Source:* Walkscore.com

this issue in chapter 10, but for now let's focus on the services that the other 99 percent ride: the fixed services.

## PERSONAL MOBILITY: THE FREEDOM TO MOVE

In 2009, we began to see web-based tools that allow you to enter an address and see where you can get to from there on transit in a fixed amount of time. Figure 1-1, for example, is the output from WalkScore.com when queried by someone near the San Francisco Civic Center at 9:00 am.[1]

These tools aren't for planning a trip; rather, they're for visualizing your freedom. That freedom is transit's product. The core product that arises from transit is personal mobility, by which I mean *the freedom to move beyond your walking range*. Mobility is a controversial concept, so it's worth taking a moment to clarify how I'll use the term and why. Readers who are less interested in theory may skip the rest of this chapter, but anyone who thinks theoretically about transportation or urbanism will find this section crucial.

## More on Personal Mobility

For more thorough discussion of the concept of personal mobility and how it relates to prevailing concepts of mobility and access in urban planning theory, see http://www.humantransit.org/01box.html.

A quick survey of definitions of mobility turns up a range of slightly different ones, indicating some ambiguity in the word. Here are a few:

The condition of moving freely.[2]

Ease of moving about.[3]

Movement of people or goods within the transportation system.[4]

By defining the term *personal mobility* as a freedom, I mean something close to "ease of moving about," but this is not at all the same as *movement*. The first describes a degree of freedom, while the second is a result of some people choosing to exercise that freedom.

If you think of *person movement* as transit's product, as many conventional measures do, the output of transit that matters is passenger-miles or passenger-kilometers. A passenger-mile is one passenger carried for 1 mile. (Fifty passenger miles, for example, could mean one passenger carried for 50 miles, or 50 passengers each carried for 1 mile.) As an approach to measuring transit's output, this concept of quantities of movement is troublesome. It doesn't measure how readily people got to where they were going; it just measures how far they were moved. Most of the time, though, our travel isn't motivated by a sheer desire for movement; it's motivated by the need to do something—to make some kind of economic or personal contact—that is too far away to walk to. In most cases, we don't want movement. We want access.

*Access* is the ability to complete some desired personal or economic transaction. Your mobility can be visualized as where you can go in a given time. Access is how many useful or valuable things you can do. If a new grocery store opens near your house, that addition doesn't improve your mobility but it does improve your access. You can now get your groceries closer to home, so you don't need as much mobility as you did before. You can also improve your access (but not your mobility) by working at home instead of commuting, downloading music instead of going to a store, or moving in with your romantic partner. In other words, much of the work of access is about eliminating the need to move your body around the city in order to complete the economic and personal transactions that make up a life.

As Todd Litman[5] points out, access can be achieved in three ways. You can (1) travel to the thing you need, in which case you need mobility; you can (2) obtain it via telecommunications; or you can (3) relocate either yourself or the desired thing so that both are closer together. Urban re-development, which adds new destinations close to you, supports option 3 at a large scale.

Transit plays a role in both option 1 and option 3. Transit provides mobility directly, but it can also influence urban development, which in turn can improve access. For example, if a new subway station opens near your house, you get improved mobility. But if the station leads to new development around it, you may get a new grocery store close to home. Even if you never ride transit, that's an access improvement for you.

Still, transit's role in mobility is direct, whereas its influence on redevelopment is indirect. Transit may lead to access-improving development, but only via several intermediate and unreliable steps. You can build a transit line and still not get new development if any of several other things don't fall into place—including zoning, economic growth, cooperative neighbors, courageous developers, and bankers willing to lend. In that case, the new transit project doesn't improve access at all, unless it has improved the first kind of access: mobility.

So personal mobility—the freedom to move—is the direct product of public transit. Mobility doesn't always generate movement, but it does generate happiness. For this reason, people will resist locating in places where it seems to be denied.

If we want cities to be built in ways that require less travel—that is, if we want cities with better access—we will need to ensure that those cities still have generous transit mobility. We need to show that if you locate in a transit-intensive place, you will be able to get to lots of places that matter to you, on transit.

So in a book on transit, I'm going to insist that personal mobility—the freedom to move—is still transit's primary product. Again, mobility is only one dimension of access. The other two are urban redevelopment and telecommunications, both of which can reduce the need for travel. But mobility is the kind of access that most people expect transit, in particular, to deliver.

Chapter 14 will look more at urban form and all the ways we can change it, but we can't use transit to create better cities unless we first understand how transit does its primary task of providing personal mobility. Transit must focus not just on city-building impacts but also on the perspective of someone who needs to go somewhere, and get there soon, to address an immediate need. This person isn't thinking about how better transit might help transform the city, but rather, "I need to be there!" We must figure out whether transit can help, and if so, how.

# 2

# WHAT MAKES TRANSIT USEFUL? SEVEN DEMANDS AND HOW TRANSIT SERVES THEM

If you spend any time inside the offices of a transit agency, you get used to seeing messages like "The customer comes first!" and "Service is our business!" Posted in the elevator or in the lunchroom, these messages are supposed to focus employees on a particular mission called "service."

But what kind of service do we need to provide so that people will use it? What is this mysterious thing called "service" anyway?

The most common answer is "Ask the customer!" As in any business, transit customers have needs, desires, and dislikes that must be a starting point in designing and operating a transit system. Most transit agencies do listen to public comments and demands and sometimes change direction because of them.

But most public comments are narrow and self-interested. A person wants transit to stop in a particular place, or not to, because of their personal needs or desires, not because it will help make the system more useful to the entire community.

To plan service for a whole community, including the vast majority who never comment, effective network planners look beyond self-interested demands and think more broadly about what motivates people to use transit. This doesn't mean substituting our judgment for the customer's, but it does mean trying to discern underlying patterns in the diverse comments that agencies receive, and thinking about how various service changes would improve transit's ability to attract riders and fit the larger goals of the city or region it serves.

## OUR SEVEN DEMANDS

In the hundreds of hours I've spent listening to people talk about their transit needs, I've heard seven broad expectations that potential riders have of a transit service that they would consider riding:

1. It takes me *where* I want to go.
2. It takes me *when* I want to go.
3. It is a good use of my *time*.
4. It is a good use of my *money*.
5. It *respects* me in the level of safety, comfort, and amenity it provides.
6. I can *trust* it.
7  It gives me *freedom* to change my plans.

I've listed the demands in the order in which you, as a customer, usually evaluate them. Generally, you would first evaluate transit in terms of whether it exists at all in the place where you need it (demand 1). Then you would consult a schedule and determine whether it's there *when* you need it (demand 2). Next, you might compare the cost of transit (in money and time) with the benefits (demands 3 and 4) to decide whether transit is worth trying compared to your alternatives.

Now you are ready to try the service. You notice whether you feel comfortable and respected as a passenger, and whether you can put your travel time to good use (demand 5). If you become a regular customer, you start noticing whether the service works the same way day after day—in short, you decide whether you can trust it (demand 6).

Finally, as your own needs vary from day to day, you begin to discover how well the service responds to those changes (demand 7). Can you get home, or to school, in the middle of the day to tend to a sick child? Can you, on the spur of the moment, stop off at a cinema and see a movie, knowing that it is still possible to get home 3 hours later? Can you quickly figure out how to make other trips elsewhere in the city, to visit friends across town, or to attend medical appointments, or to go shopping? In short, does the transit system help you to feel free—able to enjoy all the riches of your city in a spontaneous way?

These seven demands, then, are dimensions of the mobility that transit provides. They don't yet tell us how good we need the service to be, but they will help us identify the kinds of goodness we need to care about. In short, we can use these as a starting point for defining *useful* service.

## Side Issues and Side Effects

Do these demands encompass everything that people ask of their transit agencies? Of course not. There are two other important categories of demands.

First, a transit agency hears feedback about how the agency functions as an employer, as a company, and as a corporate citizen. Such issues include fairness to workers, discrimination, sponsorship of community events, donations to charities, relations with other governments, relations with the media, and so forth. These are all important, but they are common to all agencies and companies within a community, regardless of their product, so focusing on these will distract us from understanding public transit in particular. For that reason, I will set these aside for this book's purpose. You don't need to understand transit to understand these issues.

Second, agencies get many comments about the side effects of their equipment and facilities, and these considerations are enormous factors in decisions about new transit infrastructure. The big side effects of transit are emissions, noise, vibration, and the way various transit vehicles affect the look and feel of the urban environment. Many of these are huge issues, and a great deal of money is spent mitigating these impacts. But these comments aren't about the basic work of public transit, either. An especially noisy and polluting bus has the same impact regardless of whether it's a public transit bus or a tour bus; in fact, the same bus may serve either purpose. Other technologies attract advocacy because of positive side effects. Streetcars, for example, are popular in part because of how they look and feel in the urban streetscape.

In considering side effects, we need to think about transit the way we think about the fire department. Firefighting has lots of side effects, including the space the big trucks require and the noise of their sirens. Now and then, those effects become so objectionable that people complain about them, and fire departments have to respond to those complaints, as they should. So there's a values trade-off here, an example of the plumber's question: Should we reduce the effectiveness of firefighting a little in order to mitigate some of its impacts?

Still, all sides of debates around firefighting impacts can see that there is a job called "firefighting" that is the defining purpose of these companies. That doesn't mean that it's the only thing that matters or that its efficiency should be ranked above all of its other impacts. But discussions about impacts usually reflect a shared understanding that the firefighters' main job is to put out fires and that everyone has an interest in seeing that job done well.

When it comes to transit, the balance of power in these conversations is different. Not everyone recognizes that transit has a defining activity—personal mobility that does not require personal vehicles—and that a transit agency has to maintain a primary focus on that even as it tries to manage its side effects. Side effects are important, but they should not create confusion about the defining mission of transit, which is to provide personal mobility. The seven demands for useful service are all about that mission.

## THE ELEMENTS OF USEFUL SERVICE

So how does transit meet the seven demands that we identified above? How do we translate the demands into specific things that transit agencies have to provide and measure? Figure 2-1 shows how each of the seven demands relates to the key measurable features of a transit service. Don't worry if it looks complicated. We'll step through the key points. Still, you may find it useful for reference as we explore how the various transit concepts are connected.

### Demand 1: "It Takes Me *Where* I Want to Go"

The first demand—"it takes me *where* I want to go"—involves two key measurable features of a transit system:

First, the location of *stops and stations* determines how close transit service comes to each place that anyone might want to come from or go to.

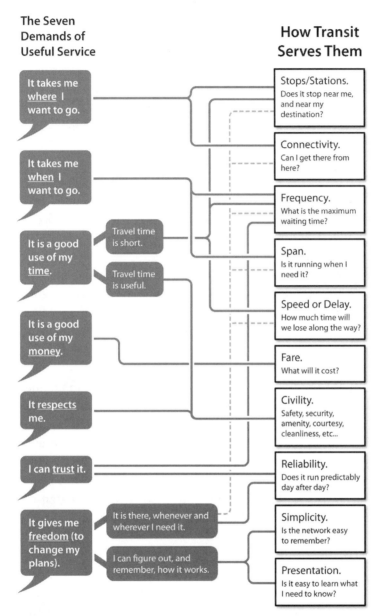

**Figure 2-1** Seven desires for useful transit, and how transit serves them. *Credit:* Eric Orozco

We'll discuss stops and stations in chapter 5, and the lines that they form in chapter 4.

Second, *connectivity* is a measure of whether transit links the place you want to go (your *destination*) with the place you are now (your *origin*). Stops near your origin and destination do not guarantee connectivity: a transit agency may serve both point A and point B but be unable to take you from A to B by a reasonably direct path. Chapters 12 and 13 explore connectivity.

## Demand 2: "It Takes Me *When* I Want To Go"

The second demand also encompasses two measurable features.

First is the question of whether transit runs at all when you need it; the answer to this is the *span* of service. Span is indicated by the scheduled time of the first and last trip in each direction.

Next is the question of whether the service runs often enough that you can leave when you really want to go. The measure of how often transit runs is *frequency*. Frequency is usually described by the number of minutes between consecutive trips, so—as in golf—lower scores are better. A service that runs every 15 minutes, for example, is twice as useful, and twice as expensive to operate, as one that runs every 30 minutes.

This number—the gap between consecutive trips in minutes—is called the *headway*. If we change a frequency from every 30 minutes to every 15 minutes, we say that we've doubled the frequency by halving the headway. Again, when you hear the term *high frequency*, that means a *low* headway, such as service every 10 minutes or less. A high headway, such as 60 minutes, is a low frequency.

Frequency is one of the most misunderstood concepts in transit. We'll return to it often throughout the book, especially in chapter 7.

## Demand 3: "It Is a Good Use of My *Time*"

Demand 3 includes all the ways of making travel time useful to the passenger. These efforts can involve providing reading lights, electrical outlets, phones, Internet access, and other facilities that enable a passenger to work, sleep, or do something else valuable while waiting and riding.

Still, we want travel time to be short. Travel time is one of the most critical elements of a passenger's decision about whether to use transit routinely, and for this reason, the models that predict ridership give it huge weight.

When we think of saving time, we usually think of speed. When we're driving, the average speed that we'll achieve is the measure of how fast we'll cover the distance to our desired destination. When people who usually by travel by car think about a transit issue, they often focus on how fast the vehicles can physically go.

But for transit, the vehicle speed is a small part of the picture. What matters is how much time it takes to complete an *entire* desired trip. So to understand this demand, we have to look in more detail at all the phases of a trip and the potential for delay involved with each. We'll come back to that at the end of this chapter, and we'll dissect speed further in chapter 8.

## Demand 4: "It Is a Good Use of My *Money*"

This fourth demand is relatively simple, since *fares* are the primary monetary cost of transit use. People compare the cost of using transit with the cost of getting somwhere in some other way, and this can strongly influence their decision. Chapter 11 explores fares.

## Demand 5: "It *Respects* Me"

At its core, the fifth demand is about whether the rider feels valued as a customer, as a citizen, and as a human being. Obviously, this demand is so subjective that it could come apart into a million values.

Fortunately, most of us do agree on some things that contribute to our sense of being respected. For example, comfort, courtesy, safety, and security all signify we are valued as human beings and as customers. Some of these features also help to give value to our time, so they follow also from the third demand.

All of these values fall under a large category that I'll call *civility*. These values are not about transit's ability to transport us but, rather, about its ability to treat us like human beings while it is doing so. By "civility," I mean widely shared values unrelated to travel time or cost—such as comfort, cleanliness, courtesy, safety, security, and amenities that give value to our time.

Although they can't all be quantified, the elements of civility in transit are, by definition, widely agreed upon within a culture. Everyone understands the importance of comfort, cleanliness, courtesy, safety, and security. Some level of civility is essential if we are to carry a diverse range of customers. When a transit system gets the reputation of being "only for poor people," despite good speed and frequency, it is often because its civility has fallen so low that most people don't consider using it as an option. Often, by this time, other important values will have declined as well, because the only people who care about them are politically powerless.

Definitions of civility may vary from one culture to the next. In some cultures, for example, civility may include separate seating areas for men and women. The acceptable standard for certain elements of civility may also vary by culture. Passenger railways in India may not offer the personal space and comfort that a North American visitor would expect, but they do meet the expectations that prevail in India, so they're popular. Civility includes, by definition, whatever expectations are widely shared within the culture.

Civility is hugely important, and problems in this area often send signals that a transit system is uninterested in serving the whole community. Still, the work of creating civility in transit is not much different from what it is in other endeavors. The customer service skills of a merchant, for example, are easily transferred to the customer-contact role of a transit information agent or, for that matter, a bus driver. Creating a civilized waiting environment for transit is not that different from designing waiting areas for other businesses and government functions. So, this is an area where we can rely on expertise from other fields, and indeed much good work is being done on the topic. For that reason, in a book that focuses on transit in particular, I won't discuss civility in great detail.

## Demand 6: "I Can *Trust* It"

Your transit service may get you to work on time 90 percent of the time, but if you're going to a meeting that's crucial for your career, you might not want to risk the one-in-ten chance that it will let you down. Our ability to trust a transit operation is called *reliability*, though frequency is also an important aspect of trust because it reduces our dependence on the reliability of any single transit vehicle.

### Demand 7: "It Gives Me *Freedom* (to Change My Plans)"

Freedom is a crucial sensation, and in most places it is the private car's crowning virtue. When limited transit schedules interfere with people's lives—forcing them, for example, to decline a last-minute dinner invitation or cut short the family's day at the zoo—we see why transit is not the mode of choice for more of the trips we make.

In transit, the real test of freedom is spontaneity. Can I change my plans suddenly? Can I get home if I need to, or to my child's school if something comes up? Can I simply move freely around my city, following whatever impulse I may feel at the moment? Some transit systems approach that level of convenience, at least in dense cities. In some of those same cities, you'll find that your car is an encumbrance. If you've ever been stuck in traffic on a busy downtown street while pedestrians and cyclists flow past you and subway trains zoom beneath you, you know that sometimes your car can become your prison.

If anything, the demand for spontaneity is increasing as families diversify. In the United States, for example, most households no longer have a parent devoted solely to the home; the norm is increasingly a couple who both work or a single working parent. These people have complex lives in which "something may come up" during the day that requires unexpected travel. Corporate styles are demanding more self-management and accountability from their employees, which often means that employees may go to work in the morning without knowing exactly when they'll come home.

This demand for spontaneity is met mostly by values that we've already listed. A transit system offers freedom if it offers *frequency* and *span* (so that there is service whenever you suddenly need it) and a reasonable average *speed* compared to your alternatives. We might think of these values as "squared" by their role in meeting the demand for freedom in addition to their role in meeting one of our other basic demands.

But freedom is also the biggest payoff of *legibility*. Only if you can remember the layout of your transit system and how to navigate it can you use transit to move spontaneously around your city. Legibility has two parts: (1) simplicity in the design of the network, so that it's easy to explain and remember, and (2) the clarity of the presentation in all the various media.

No amount of brilliant presentation can compensate for an overly complicated network. Anyone who has looked at a confusing tangle of routes on a system map and decided to take their car can attest to how complexity can undermine ridership. Good network planning tries to create the simplest possible network. Where complexity is unavoidable, other legibility tools help customers to see through the complexity and to find patterns of useful service that may be hidden there. For example, chapter 7 explores the idea of Frequent Network maps, which enable you to see just the lines where service is coming soon, all day. These, it turns out, are not just a navigation tool, but also a land use planning tool.

Another important legibility technique is to minimize the difference between the transit network and the street network, the latter of which you can assume your customers already know. Suppose you're in San Francisco and see a bus whose overhead sign says "38: GEARY 48th Ave." If you live in San Francisco, you probably know where Geary Boulevard and 48th Avenue are. So just a glance at this sign tells you that there's a bus that runs out Geary as far as 48th. The sign gives everyone who sees it a full sense of what the service does and how it might be useful. Clear information is often the best marketing.

This legibility is not the result of just a well-phrased sign. It's also the result of planners deciding that it's best for transit to just run the length of Geary Boulevard, rather than branch off of it in complicated ways that could never be described or remembered so easily.

As for maps and schedules, these used to be the transit agency's job, but the role is shifting to the private sector. Many transit agencies are now releasing their route and schedule data in standard formats, so that anyone can design printed maps or online applications to present it. This is a welcome change. There's no reason you should rely on a transit agency for maps and schedules, any more than you would rely on your government's highway department for maps of the highway network. Presentation of real-time information, which shows actual locations of vehicles rather than just what's scheduled, is also migrating to the private sector, where entrepreneurs are competing to create mobile phone software that will present this information quickly and compellingly.

Legibility may seem like a minor problem compared to the others. For people who use transit only for the same trip every day, legibility is not a problem; you just learn how to make your routine trip and ignore all the other complexities. But if you want transit to be a primary transport mode for your city, then you want passengers to use transit for many purposes, not just a regular trip, and in this case the legibility of the system becomes a critical value. Anyone who has spent 15 minutes on hold waiting for a transit system's information line (and who only called because the maps, schedules, and website were not helpful) knows that the lack of legibility really does add to travel time and crushes any sensation of freedom.

## What It Costs

Journalists love to quote the eye-popping numbers for the construction cost of major transit lines, but *operating cost* is the eternal reality that governs most transit budgets. If you don't understand the essence of operating cost, you won't understand planning proposals.

In general, operating cost roughly doubles if you

- double the total length of the transit lines you operate, either by extending existing lines or by creating new ones;
- double frequency, for example, by cutting the headway from 30 to 15 minutes; or
- double the duration of service, for example, by expanding from 8 hours a day to 16 hours a day.

But one popular improvement saves operating cost: increasing speed. In general, if you were able to cut the travel time of a service in half—that is, double its average speed—your operating cost would drop by up to half. That's because most operating cost is labor, so it varies with time rather than distance. Run faster, and you use labor more efficiently.

For more on operating cost, see http://www.humantransit.org /02box.html. For now, remember: route distance, frequency, and span all *cost,* but speed *saves.*

## THE SEVEN PHASES OF A TRIP

Another useful way to sort the elements of useful service is to think about how they relate to the phases of a transit trip. Any trip on transit has the following phases or steps, and in each one we seek both an efficient use of our time and money and a civilized experience.

1.  *Understanding.* First, you must form a sufficient understanding of the service, frequency, and fare to know how to make the trip. This is the role of *legibility* as discussed earlier.
2.  *Accessing (at the origin).* You then walk, drive, or cycle to the stop or station where you will board the service. Here, there are limits to what your transit agency can do, apart from locating the stop at a logical place, making it a civilized place to wait, and providing parking options for your car or bike, where appropriate. Other than this, you're at the mercy of the city's street network and development pattern.
3.  *Waiting.* Waiting is everyone's least favorite phase of a trip. It's governed mostly by *frequency* and *reliability*, but of course the quality of the waiting environment has a big impact. Waiting is also being transformed in interesting ways by personal technology, most notably by real-time information that tells you how long you have to wait.
4.  *Paying.* We think of paying as spending money, but paying can also cost time, especially if you are unfamiliar with the system. If the driver collects the fares, your act of paying takes the time of everyone already onboard. That's why higher-volume transit systems (rail, bus, or ferry) are shifting to forms of fare collection that require you to buy a ticket before you board (more on this in chapter 11).
5.  *Riding.* The time spent on the transit vehicle is governed by average speed (or *delay*) and *reliability*. The quality of the time, which is also important, is governed by both the quality of the vehicle and your ability to make use of the time, often through personal technology. Chapter 8 explores these issues.
6.  *Connecting.* If your trip requires a connection, you'll repeat steps 2 through 5 for that connection. Minimizing the hassle of these steps is the work of *connectivity*, as we'll explore in Chapter 12. For example, fare systems that offer free connections eliminate the cost and hassle of repeating step 4.

7. *Accessing (at the destination)*. Finally, you'll repeat step 2 in reverse, traveling by some means from the transit stop/station to your actual destination. Again, the location of *stops/stations* (chapter 5) is the main transit feature that governs this access, but the design of the local area, which is usually outside a transit agency's control, is also a major impact.

Notice again that frequency appears multiple times. Frequency rules step 3 (waiting) and counts again in step 6 if a connection is required. But frequency also plays a big role in step 1 (understanding). A very frequent transit service is one where you don't worry about a timetable, and that's a huge step toward making understanding easier.

## How Much Does Each Phase Matter?

The phases of a trip raise an important question that's likely to have a very personal answer: Do you just want to minimize your total travel time? Or, do you dislike certain phases of the trip so much that you'd endure a longer trip in order to minimize them? (Some of us might also endure a longer trip in order to have a particular pleasure, such as a ride on a vehicle that they perceive as fun, but this is even harder to quantify, as the nature of fun is so subjective and variable.)

Many studies have looked at how different kinds of delay seem to influence people's decisions to use transit, mostly for the purposes of ridership prediction. There are many ways to frame this question, but the most useful for our purposes is: "How much does a minute of this time deter someone from riding, as compared to the deterrent effect of a minute of riding time?" Table 2-1 shows some figures cited in an influential US manual, derived from studies in eight North American cities dating from 1960 to 1995.[1]

For example, when Table 2-1 says that walk time is weighted, on average, at 2.2 times riding time, we mean that 1 minute of walking time has as much deterrent effect as 2.2 minutes of riding time in determining whether someone will choose to use transit. For an extreme but simple example, if you could get to your destination in either 10 minutes of pure walking or 20 minutes of pure riding (with no wait or walk delay), these models say that, on average, people would rather have the 20-minute ride, even though they'd get to their destination 10 minutes later.

**Table 2-1** Deterrent Effect of Various Kinds of Travel Time
(relative to ride time = 1)

| Delay Type: | Walk | Initial Wait | Ride | Wait for Connection |
|---|---|---|---|---|
| *Governing Feature:* | *Stops, Stations (chapter 5)* | *Frequency (chapter 7)* | *Speed, Delay (chapter 8)* | *Frequency, Connections (chapters 7, 12)* |
| Minimum | 0.8 | 0.8 | 1.0 | 1.1 |
| Average | 2.2 | 2.1 | 1.0 | 2.5 |
| Maximum | 4.4 | 5.1 | 1.0 | 4.4 |

*Source: Transit Capacity and Qualiy of Service Manual, 2nd ed.*

When you put it that simply, it's easy to say, "Wait, but I wouldn't do that!" Factors like these have to be used with care. They're the result of observing many people's travel behavior in complicated situations where many motivations overlap, so an observed behavior that appears to be a response to waiting time may actually be about something else, such as the quality of the waiting environment, the reliability of the service, or the availability of information. Analyses like the one discussed here are often cited as reasons why transit planners shouldn't expect customers to walk, or to make a connection, even if that makes their trip faster. But look at the minimums! All of these types of delay have, in various situations, been reduced to around 1.0. Achieving that would mean that for most people in most situations, all the elements of travel time are equally tolerable. That, in turn, would mean that with a manageable number of exceptions, the total door-to-door trip time, compared to the customer's alternatives, could be viewed as the main kind of time that matters to ridership.[a] If that were

---

[a] There will always be exceptions, but there can also be continuous efforts toward addressing those exceptions, efforts made simpler by a clearer goal. Right now, many people commuting long distances value a good on-board work environment, but wireless internet and smartphones will eventually improve the working environment on most long-distance transit services. Weather deters walking and waiting sometimes, but this can be addressed through weather-protected connection points, heated or cooled shelters, and the continuous awnings that some cities (such as rainy Wellington, New Zealand) require in business districts. If enabling people to get where they're going as

true, it would be much easier to decide, for example, that most people will walk farther to a faster service that will get them to their destination sooner. Suddenly, technical debates about transit would become exponentially simpler.

Is that possible? If it were our objective, we could certainly get much closer than we are now. Chapters 5 (on stop spacing), 7 (on frequency), and 12 (on connections) will look at these three kinds of travel time and how we can minimize their deterrent effect. Of course, we also have to care about in-vehicle travel time, which is the subject of chapter 8.

But there's another reason for optimism about bringing down the deterring effects of walking, waiting, and connecting, and that is today's revolution in information, which is not reflected in these twentieth-century figures. Most of these figures, for example, were developed in the absence of trip planning software, which allows you to evaluate your own transit options for a trip and decide for yourself if you prefer a longer trip that avoids walking or connecting. Without that knowledge, many passengers may have navigated by habit rather than choice because the available information encouraged that.

Real-time information is also transformative. Walking, waiting, and connecting are all made worse by uncertainty. Think about how different a walk to the bus or streetcar stop will feel if you know that the vehicle you want will be there in exactly 9 minutes. Even if you're in a hurry to reach your destination, you won't need to hurry while walking, so you'll enjoy the walk more. Waiting and connecting, too, become less onerous if you know the exact length of the wait, so that you can do other things with your time.

As mobile phone–based information sources become more sophisticated and universal, we will see a decline in uncertainty. Eventually, we may well reach a point where the length of the whole trip is really the only duration that matters. With clear, immediate, and reliable information, won't people find it easier, when they're in a hurry, to choose the fastest way?

---

fast as possible were the objective, a great many available innovations—in urban design, information systems, and network planning—could be brought to bear, and new innovation would have a clearer goal to pursue.

# 3

# FIVE PATHS TO CONFUSION

Throughout this book, you'll find examples of common misunderstandings about transit. In each case, my goal is not just to refute them but to suggest why they are so common and understandable, so that we can forgive and correct these mistakes both in others and in ourselves. A lively transit debate may seem to reflect many kinds of confusion, but we can penetrate the chaos by noticing a few common themes.

## MAP-READING ERRORS

During their television coverage of the 2010 US election night, CNN repeatedly called the viewer's attention to a map of the United States in which the congressional districts were colored red for Republicans or blue for Democrats. Each time, we were shown the map showing the pre-2010 makeup of Congress. Then the reporter said, "Now, watch this!" As he waved his hand, the map changed to show the post-2010 makeup, with many blue areas changed to red. We were meant to perceive a vast Republican wave pouring across the nation.

CNN was asking us to make the most common of all map-reading errors: *perceiving map area as though it were population*. The visual impression that a map makes comes from the sizes of areas on the map; a big zone looks more important than a small zone, even though, if the zones are congressional districts, both represent the same number of voters.

While the Republicans picked up many seats in 2010, CNN's map visually exaggerated those gains because only rural and outer-suburban districts are big enough to show up on a national map. Many outer-suburban districts, which often include extensive rural areas and therefore show up as big, tend to be close to the political center, so they frequently flip in elections. Many of them turned from blue to red in 2010, and it was these districts that created most of the CNN map's apparent "red wave." The same map would have shown an equally exaggerated "blue wave" for the Democrats two years earlier.

What you cannot see on a national map are the many districts that are inside of urban areas. They are too small in area to see unless you zoom into them, which CNN didn't. I am not sure if CNN's emphasis on this map was malice or foolishness, but it certainly showed how easy it is to misread map area as population, and thus form a distorted impression of what is occurring.

Transit planning requires looking at maps of data about populations, so you will encounter many opportunities to make this mistake. Suppose you're looking at a map showing the rate of zero-car households in a city. On the edge of the city is a huge zone that's all wilderness except for six recluses living in mobile homes deep in the woods, four of whom have cars. That's a 33 percent rate of zero-car households, and the whole vast zone will show up as having one of the most extreme rates of carlessness in the city. In fact, this large, brightly colored zone may be the most prominent thing on the map. Some people viewing this map may think: How terrible! We clearly need transit out there! The antidote to this map-reading error is to keep asking: "Wait, how many *people* are we talking about?" In this example, the answer is two.

In chapter 7, we'll encounter a similar map-reading error when it comes to looking at maps of transit service. Briefly, most transit maps show the paths that transit runs on but not how frequently it runs. As a result, they tend to conceal the patterns of good service, which tend also to be the patterns of good ridership. So when looking at a transit map, you may need to say: "Wait, these are just routes. What are the frequencies? How late do they run? In other words, how much actual service am I looking at here?"

## MOTORIST'S ERRORS

A *motorist's error* is any mistake that arises from unconsciously thinking about transit as though it works just like cars and roads.[a] These errors often come up when people who usually travel by car find themselves making decisions about transit. Understandably, they tend to think about transit as an analogy to the mode of transport that they know. Many people who drive are strong transit supporters, and they can still make good transit decisions, but it helps to be aware of this risk and consciously correct for it.

Many such errors are obvious. Someone who has never tried to walk along a busy street as a pedestrian, for example, may not grasp why such a walk could be unsafe or intolerable, and what might need to be done to fix that problem. That's an example of an obvious difference between motoring and transit, one that most people can easily notice and correct for.

But the pervasive motorist's errors are more subtle. The most common is overvaluing speed and undervaluing frequency, because speed is meaningful to a motorist's experience while frequency really isn't. Roads are there whenever you need them, so there is no road equivalent of the transit concept of waiting time. The closest thing to frequency that most motorists experience is the cycling of traffic signals, but this is not a close analogy at all, since each signal delay is rarely more than 2 minutes. Transit riders, by contrast, may face major waits at the beginning of a trip or at a connection point. For them, waiting time—that is, frequency—is often the major variable that governs actual travel time. We'll come back to this motorist's error in chapters 7 and 8.

## BOX ERRORS AND FALSE DICHOTOMIES

Sometimes, we're tempted to think about a *spectrum* as though it were a series of box-like *categories*. If you and a friend disagree about whether something is blue or purple, you're making this error together. Blue and purple

---

[a] To be fair, these errors can be made by anyone who rides transit rarely but frequently pilots a vehicle down a road, including cyclists. I call these motorist's errors only because motorists tend to dominate political discussion in many cities and are most likely to be unaware of how their motoring experience may affect their transit thinking.

are adjacent zones on a continuous spectrum of colors (technically, wavelengths of light), and zones on a spectrum can only have fuzzy or arbitrary edges. So if you disagree about whether something is blue or purple, you can both be right, based on slightly different notions of where you mark the boundary in the fuzzy area where blue shades into purple. If one of you is right and the other wrong, it can only be because of some arbitrary standard about where blue ends and purple begins, a standard you've both agreed to respect.

Color is really a spectrum, but our language makes the spectrum hard to talk about. Our category words feel like boxes with hard edges: blue, purple, tall, wealthy. They invite us to say "Jim is tall," and to assume that this statement must be true or false. But like colors, most category words really refer to directions or zones on a continuous spectrum. There's no objective basis for saying, "Jim is tall," unless we just mean, "Jim is taller than most people." "Tall" is not a box; it's just a range or direction on a spectrum of possible heights. We all know that, and for simple ideas like height or color this error rarely causes trouble.

But when we talk about emotive categories, such as wealth or success, we can easily lose sight of the spectrum, and as with blue and purple, this can cause pointless arguments. Consider a famous comment widely (if falsely) attributed to former British prime minister Margaret Thatcher: A man who, beyond the age of 26, finds himself on a bus can count himself as a failure.[1] Stated that way, "a failure" sounds like a box that you're either in or out of. Associating buses with failure or poverty is a common attitude in certain cities. If you think about failure or poverty as a box, this can be an easy way to decide that buses aren't worth your attention and that there's no point in thinking about how buses and rail transit can work together as one network.

But even if it's true that bus riders are poorer than rail riders on average, you can change your perspective by reminding yourself that the boundaries of "poor" and "middle class" and "wealthy" are as fuzzy or arbitrary as the boundary between blue and purple.

When a box error divides the spectrum into just two categories, it's called a *false dichotomy*. For example, you may sometimes hear transportation experts divide all transit riders into two boxes. One box, called a *discretionary* or *choice* rider, contains people who have the option of driving, and who will use transit only if it outcompetes their car. In the other box is the *transit-dependent* or *captive* rider, who has no viable alternative and therefore has to use transit. Dividing up riders this way leads to the idea that transit must compete for choice riders, while captive riders will ride no matter how poor the service gets.

These categories are imposed on reality, not derived from it. Transit dependence, like wealth itself, is a spectrum, with vast numbers of people in gray areas between "choice" and "captive." For example, many people with low incomes own a car out of necessity but experience owning a car as a financial burden. If we give these people credible alternatives to car ownership, they can experience the result as *liberating*, even though some transportation planners will now call them *captives*. Often they will find better things to spend that money on, such as education. Many people are in situations like these, and we can achieve both environmental and social good by giving them the option to own fewer cars. The two-box model of society, where everyone is either choice or captive, prevents us from seeing those possibilities.

## POLARIZATION ERRORS

Throughout this book, I will be like your plumber, asking, "Do you want more of this or more of that? You have to choose." This isn't always what you want to hear. People develop a range of responses to these questions, some of them unpleasant for the plumber.

One of the most common responses is to accuse me of advocating a particular answer to the question simply because I've stated the question. For example, if I describe some of the trade-offs between rail and bus options in a particular place, and try to do so with some equanimity, rail advocates may decide that I'm a bus advocate. If you already know where you are on a question, it can feel threatening for me to point out that there is a spectrum of credible opinions and that there are other possible valid positions on that spectrum.

I call this a polarization error, because ultimately it implies a stance of "you're either with us or against us." The polarization error is really an extreme example of a box error or false dichotomy. The speaker insists that his way of dividing the world into two boxes is the only one that's meaningful and that everyone else must judge reality on those terms.

There are some issues where I can describe the spectrum only by taking a position on it, because most people now occupy a different position out of sheer habit. For example, when we turn to the question of "connections or complexity?" in chapter 12, I will come down firmly on the side of encouraging connections in order to have a simpler network. I'll do this, though, because you don't need me to lay out the opposite position; distaste for connections, or "transfers" as Americans call them, is everywhere, and many transit systems work hard to avoid them. The notion that "people hate to transfer" is already well established, so the only way I can usefully show the spectrum of possibility is to explain in some detail why a network that requires transferring might actually be desirable. Still, "connections or complexity?" is a plumber's question, a choice between two things that we value, so there's no technically right answer. When a client agency chooses connection avoidance as the goal, in full understanding of the consequences of that choice, I'm happy to help the client design a network that serves those values.

In some situations, polarization is unavoidable. Most commonly, once you're engaged in a debate about whether to build a particular transit line, you're likely to hear polarizing comments coming from both sides. People who are committed strongly to one position will tend to hear what you say as either "for" or "against." That's one reason to think about transit more generally before you get into the middle of those debates, so that you can see both your own values and their relationship to other possible values that people might rationally hold. This book tries to lay out some of this landscape of choices so that you can find your own home in it.

## UNFORTUNATE CONNOTATIONS

Finally, many of the words that we use to talk about transit can carry troublesome connotations. We've already seen one: *captive*. I may understand that my elderly aunt can't drive and thus depends on transit, but I'll still bristle to hear her described as the transit system's captive.

Most of the words used in the transit business also have a more common meaning outside that context. The common meaning forms a connotation that hangs around the word, often causing confusion, when we use the word to talk about transit. So when choosing what words to use, it's important to think about each word's everyday meaning, not just its transit meaning.

In the next chapter, for example, we'll need a word for the path traced by a transit vehicle. This word is sometimes *route* and sometimes *line*. Which should we use? Listen to the common meaning of these two words.

When a package or message is going through a postal system, we say it's being routed. The person who delivers newspapers to subscribers in the morning is following a paper route. School buses typically follow routes. Explorers trace a route to the South Pole.

What these meanings of the word *route* have in common is that the route isn't necessarily followed very often. A route is a place where some kind of transport event happens, but the event may be rare. It may even happen only once.

The word *line*, on the other hand, has a clear meaning from geometry: a simple, straight, one-dimensional figure. In common usage, we often use *line* for something curved, like the laugh lines and worry lines on a face, and transit lines may be curved as well. But the word *line* doesn't imply an event, as *route* does. A line is a thing that's just there, no matter what happens along it.

Lurking inside these two words, in short, is a profound difference in attitude about a transit service. Do you want to think of transit as something that's always there, that you can count on? If so, call it a *line*. We never speak of rail routes, always rail lines, and we do that because the rails are always there, suggesting a permanent and reliable thing.

If you're selling a transportation product, you obviously want people to think they can count on it. So it's not surprising that in the private sector, the word is usually *line*. Trucking and shipping companies often call themselves lines, as do most private bus companies and, of course, the airlines. This doesn't mean that all these services are really line-like—some may be quite infrequent—but the company that chose the word wants you to think of their product as something that's reliably there, as something that you can count on.

So the word *route* lowers expectations for the frequency and reliability of a service. The word *line* raises those expectations. My broad intention in this book is to raise expectations of transit rather than lower them, so I will generally use *line*. However, when I speak specifically of a service that doesn't run very frequently, I'll use *route*.

Connotations can be a nuisance. Most of the time you don't want any connotation. You just want the meaning. Unfortunately, words without connotations tend to sound evasive or bureaucratic. I could insist on saying "fixed vehicle path" instead of "route" or "line," just as I could say "nonmotorized access" when I mean walking or cycling, but you wouldn't get through this book if I did. To keep our speech vivid and engaging, we often have to use words with connotations, and do our best to choose those connotations consciously.

# 4

# LINES, LOOPS, AND LONGING

Inside every transit planning decision, and behind all the field's complexities, is a simple geometry problem. The basic tool of fixed transit is the line or route, which can be straight or bent but is still basically one-dimensional. The city that we serve, however, is largely two-dimensional. We have a toolbox full of *lines*, but we need to cover an *area*.

This problem underlies all of the challenges of network design. It also defines the basic shapes of a transit route or line, which I'll call I-shapes, U-shapes, S-shapes, and O-shapes or loops. Some readers will find this chapter elementary, but when you get mad at your transit agency for designing a line a certain way, it's helpful to think about the geometry problem that your agency is trying to solve.

## THE DIRECTNESS IMPERATIVE

If you want to get from A to B in the everyday geometry of cities, a direct line between these points is the shortest way. Shortest isn't necessarily fastest, of course, but directness is a big part of what determines travel time, and good planning values it on its own terms.

Directness is a fact of geometry, so it will always be there. Speed, by contrast, is the result of complex and often ephemeral things: weather conditions, the behavior of other travelers, fare collection methods, the overall demand for travel. Speed is worth fighting for on all of those fronts, and a few features of speed—such as the exclusive right-of-way followed by rapid

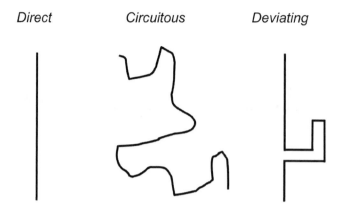

*Direct*        *Circuitous*        *Deviating*

**Figure 4-1**    Degrees of directness.

transit lines—are locked into infrastructure design in a way that makes them reliable. (We'll explore those in chapter 8.) Still, speed can change, but directness won't. So planners try to make transit as direct as it can be while still doing its job.

If a transit route is not direct, compared to the alternatives, we say it is *circuitous* (figure 4-1). A small bit of circuitousness on an otherwise direct route is called a *deviation*.

Transit planners hate deviations, because passengers riding through on the line hate them too. Deviations are more irritating than circuitous routes because they feel like broken promises. Circuitous routes never claim to be anything but circuitous; if you're in a hurry, you don't use them. But direct lines do offer the potential of being useful for people in a hurry, so adding a deviation on an otherwise direct line can defeat much of the line's purpose. Development patterns that require transit to deviate are a major problem, one that will dominate chapter 14.

Suppose we were arranging nine major activity centers to form an ideal city for various purposes. If you wanted to minimize the total distances people would need to travel between these points, you might arrange them in a square (figure 4-2).

For most other aspects of the urban economy, including minimizing the average distances that need to be traveled, the square form is better. So most urban forms have always tended to grow as two-dimensional clumps rather than along one-dimensional lines.

# Imagine a city made up of nine major points ...

This configuration would be good for minimizing total travel distances, which is why towns on open plains tend to grow this way ...

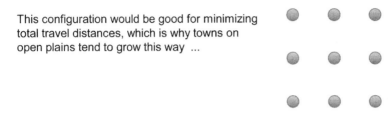

But the ideal geography for transit would be like this, so that just one line could serve them:

(Strings of towns along a coastline, for example, are easy for transit to serve.)

Given the first kind of city, what are transit's basic choices for fitting a line to a grid of dots?

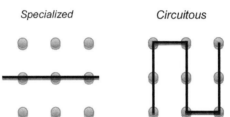

*Specialized*  *Circuitous*

We can deploy just one line, by either *specializing* (only serving certain areas) or by running a *circuitous* service

Or we can deploy *multiple* lines. It will take lots of lines to link all nine centers directly. We need fewer lines if we rely on *connections* (Chapter CXNS).

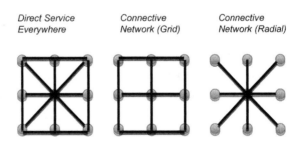

*Direct Service Everywhere*  *Connective Network (Grid)*  *Connective Network (Radial)*

*Remember! Our budget for service must be spread across the miles of line that we need to run. So fewer miles of line means more service (more frequency, longer span) on each line!*

**Figure 4-2**  Fitting a line to a city.

But suppose, just hypothetically, you were laying out a city with the intention of making transit the dominant mode—not because you should but because the example helps us see how the geometry works. In that case, the linear arrangement would be best, because that's the only arrangement where *one* transit line can be as direct as any other mode of transport could be. This is why transit has a particular advantage in urban forms that have naturally grown in a one-dimensional or linear shape, such as a string of beach towns or a barrier island or a series of villages in a mountain pass. You can serve the whole structure with a single direct line, which is the most efficient possible transit form.

## THE LINE AND THE CITY

Once a city has become two-dimensional, with important points that are not in a straight line, transit has a choice (figure 4-2).

- You can *specialize*. You can decide to serve only some of these points, so that transit can run a straight line.
- You can run a *circuitous* line, serving all the dots at the expense of not being direct between them. This is sometimes done in transit networks aiming to provide basic coverage, often for social service purposes but with no intention of competing with other alternatives.
- You can run *multiple* lines, each of which can be direct. For example, you can run a direct line between each pair of dots. Or, you can use fewer lines but make sure they connect with one another.

The third option is, of course, what's usually done. Once we have multiple lines, we face a further plumber's question: connections or complexity? If we can ask people to change from one line to another, we get a much simpler network than if we have to run direct service from every point to every other. We'll return to that question in chapter 12.

## BARRIERS AND CHOKEPOINTS

If a transit service area contains a barrier that applies to all competing forms of transport, then a transit line may bend to go through that barrier and still be called direct. The barrier can be a body of water, a mountain range, or anything else that obstructs direct travel. The limited number of points where you can cross a barrier are called *chokepoints*. For car traffic, chokepoints are a problem, but for transit, they are opportunities.

For example, in figure 4-3, a lake can be crossed by only one bridge or by going around its eastern end, so both of those points are chokepoints. All lines on this map will feel direct because every other mode of transport would have to deviate in the same way.

Chokepoints do two very useful things: First, they bring parallel lines together without deviating them. The shape of a chokepoint requires parallel lines to converge to pass through it. This creates opportunities for people to connect among these lines, thus reaching more possible destinations. If you brought parallel lines together without a chokepoint, it would feel like a deviation, but because of the chokepoint, everyone understands that all the lines are as direct as they can be. That's why chokepoints are logical sites for interchanges—places where passengers can comfortably connect between lines—a topic we'll return to in chapters 12 and 13.

Second, chokepoints allow transit-only lanes (or tracks) to offer an advantage for many different travel markets that pass through them. In figure 4-3, for example, a transit lane across the bridge would be useful for four lines, not just one, so its benefits would spread out over a large area. If

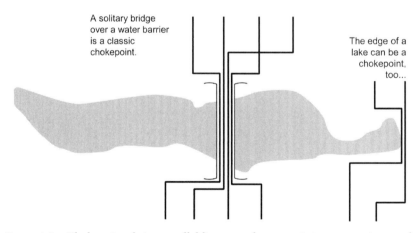

**Figure 4-3** Chokepoints bring parallel lines together, permitting connections and increasing the impact of any transit priority. *Credit:* Erin Walsh

this lane helps transit get past congestion that affects motorists through the chokepoint, it can potentially create a travel time advantage for transit for an enormous travel market.

## BASIC ROUTE SHAPES: I, U, S, AND O

Once we have a network of multiple routes, we can pursue the ideal of straightness with each line. Let's call this optimal direct line an *I-shape*, after the straight-line shape of the letter I.

Suppose, now, that we have a city of nine major centers that need to be connected to one another but arranged as in figure 4-4. There's an obvious east–west line that looks pretty direct, linking five of the nine dots. For the rest, we'll need some U-shaped lines.

A *U-shape* is designed to be reasonably direct between any two of its points *except* the endpoints. For a U-shape to work, the endpoints must be connected by a more direct I-shaped line. Of course, the system must also be based on a commitment to easy connections, an issue we'll return to in chapter 12.

If you zoom in, a portion of a U-shape can function as an I-shape. For example, the two dots in the lower right corner of the city in figure 4-4 have a useful I-shaped connection to each other, which happens to be part of a larger U-shape.

Obviously, you could also combine the two U-shaped lines together to make an S, which would perform the same functions but expand the range of dot pairs that have direct service. Transit lines that seem to meander are sometimes multiple U-shaped lines hooked together. These services are not intended to be ridden long distances but rather are meant to provide an overlapping series of short-distance links.

Finally, in the simple geometry of this chapter, U-shaped lines are literally U-shaped, but in many cases they are straight lines that are not the fastest way to travel between endpoints. For example, a local-stop bus or streetcar may follow the same path as a subway line but make far more stops. In that case, you want the subway if you're going a long distance, but the bus or streetcar is useful if you're going partway, to an area where the subway doesn't stop. In this case, the bus or streetcar line may be literally straight, but it's functionally like a U-shaped line: it's meant not to connect

Suppose that our city of nine dots looks like this ...

We might serve it with a I-shaped line and three connecting U-shaped lines:

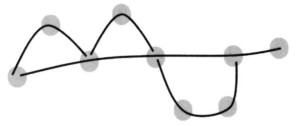

Two U-shaped lines can be combined to form an S, for more direct service.

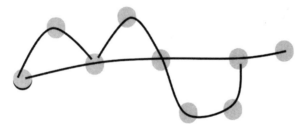

If the dots are arranged just a little differently, the two U-shapes might be combined into an O-shape, a loop.

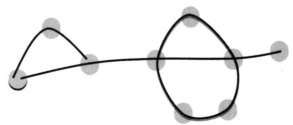

**Figure 4-4** The basic line shapes.

the endpoints but, rather, to serve the area in between, connecting it to either end.

## U-shapes and the To/Via Problem

If you're in downtown Sydney, Australia, and you want to go to the suburb of Lidcombe, do *not* take a "Lidcombe" train. That train is beginning a U-shaped routing whose far end is at Lidcombe, but as always with U-shaped lines, there's a more direct I-shaped line (which serves Lidcombe but doesn't end there) and that's the line to take.

Much of what can make transit systems bewildering—especially in vehicle and stop signage—arises from the difficulty of describing U-shaped lines clearly. To have any useful sense of where a transit service goes, you need *two* pieces of information: the "to" and the "via." The "to" is the final endpoint of the line; it's useful for telling you which direction on the line a vehicle is going. The "via" is a major intermediate stop or street or area served by the line.

A more accurate description of the "Lidcombe" train, for example, might be "to Lidcombe via Bankstown." Most people in Sydney know that if you're in the city center, Bankstown isn't on the way to Lidcombe, so these three words are enough to warn them that they're looking at a U-shaped line.

U-shaped lines exist *to serve their midpoints, not their endpoints.* If you're at the end of a U-shaped line, then you really care about the "via," because that tells you about the area that the line is designed to serve. But if you're in the middle of a U-shaped line, you care about the "to," because that tells you which direction on the line a bus, ferry, tram, or train is going. That's why good signage (on vehicles and at stops) always gives *both* "to" and "via" information. Ideal signage is even more sensitive: at endpoints of a U-shaped line, it emphasizes the "via," whereas at midpoints, it emphasizes the "to."

## LOOPS AND LONGING

Look again at figure 4-4. Let's imagine that one dot is in a slightly different place, as shown in the bottom image. This location invites us to combine

## More on the To/Via Problem

For more details and examples of the to/via problem, see http://www .humantransit.org/04box.html.

two U-shapes into an O-shape, a continuous two-way loop. But be careful. Geometrically, a loop is any path that begins and ends at the same point. If you think of the loop as continuous at that point, then a loop has no beginning or end. It's like a circle, possibly pushed into a noncircular shape but retaining the endlessness that is the essence of a circle.

When someone wants all parts of an area to be connected, and tries to express this in the language of transit, they often talk about loops. The loop is an appealing *image* because it's a thing that transit can do that seems to encompass an entire two-dimensional area with a feeling of completeness and closure. I have lost count of how many times people have explained their mobility needs to me by saying, "We need some kind of loop."

But there's a problem with loops, and it's so obvious that it's easy to forget: *very few people want to travel in circles.* Most people experience their travel desires as "I am here and I need to be there." The desire for transportation is a feeling about two points of space, "here" and "there." In the geometry of cities, the shape of that desire is a straight line connecting those points.

A series of overlapping U-shaped routes can often logically form a continuous loop. You'll find continuous loop lines in the subway systems of Moscow, Berlin, and Tokyo. And of course, all of this geometry is the same for buses as for trains. You'll find large looping bus lines in continuous orbit around some cities, including San Antonio, Brisbane, and Perth. Again, these frequent two-way loops function as an overlapping series of U-shapes; nobody with a destination in mind would need to ride more than halfway around them.

Notice, however, what loops do not do. Unlike I-shapes, loops are never a reasonably direct link between *all* of their stops, and for many pairs of stops (say, stops on opposite sides of the loop) they are quite circuitous. People are often drawn to loops because they want transit to connect a whole two-dimensional area, through some kind of ring of stops. In its completeness and closure, the loop forms an attractive *image* of how such a desire might be satisfied. But a loop does not, in fact, satisfy that desire, or at least not by itself.

Over a short distance, a loop may be as useful as a more or less I-shaped line, but sooner or later a loop must bend, and therefore be less straight, and therefore be less attractive for continuous travel. By the time you get to the opposite side of a loop from where you started, the loop's path has been substantially longer than a straight path. If you're in a big-city transit system, there's almost certainly a much more direct I-shaped route that should be used for that kind of trip.

It can be even worse. Some loops are one-way.

## The Perils of One-Way Service

Any of the route forms we've discussed can be run one-way. Some commuter rail, for example, runs on a single track, with all trains going only one way in the morning, typically into the big city, and the other way in the afternoon. Many commuter express bus lines are also one-way.

The obvious problem in these cases is that the vehicles used to run the line will pile up at the end. To be used again, they need to be returned out of service, and in any case, their drivers need to be returned to their starting points, because most driver shifts must begin and end at the same place (more on these challenges in chapter 6). This is why one-way routes are often not that much cheaper to operate than two-way routes covering the same terrain.

Loops, however, are easy to run one-way. In fact, a two-way loop line is usually operated as though it were two one-way loops, running continuously in opposite directions.

But if a loop runs in only one direction, you may have to ride more than halfway around the loop to get where you're going. So they work only in two settings.

First, in very low-ridership areas, such as circulation in low-density suburbs, the one-way loop is the cheapest way to cover a lot of area in a given time. These routes have a goal of providing basic lifeline access, so they sacrifice directness to cover as large an area as possible. These one-way loops can never attract a customer whose time is valuable, because they

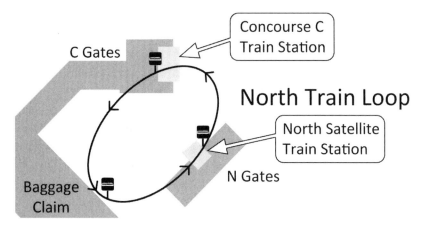

**Figure 4-5** Seattle airport shuttle loop. *Credit:* Erin Walsh

guarantee that in one direction or the other, you'll have a very circuitous trip. But where the intention is simply to provide some transit option to a low-demand area at minimal cost, these loops may have a role.

The other application for one-way loops is in very small circulation networks, such as in an airport or downtown, where the whole loop is so short that it doesn't matter much if you go the long way around it. In the Seattle airport, for example, trains cycle among just three stops in a continuous one-way loop (figure 4-5).

The Seattle airport trains cycle the entire loop in about 6 minutes, so a trip directly from the main terminal to the N gates is about 2 minutes, while the trip back the long way via the C gates is about 4 minutes. It's just not enough of a difference to worry about. Small-loop circulators in downtowns work the same way, including the Miami MetroMover, the Detroit People Mover, and the Sydney Monorail. Sometimes simple shuttle bus lines are designed on the same principle. Again, these very small one-way loops offer reasonable travel times because they serve just a few stations focused on a small area, so that even the long way around the loop takes only a few minutes.

## Breaking Out of Loops

Loops have other problems. An I-shaped line can easily be extended on either end without affecting the existing riders, but loops can't be extended;

a city that outgrows its loop has to break it apart, disrupting existing trips. So if an urban area is growing or changing, loops may limit the options for growth in the future.

Finally, of course, loops run with a driver raise the problem of driver breaks. An I-shaped or U-shaped line has an endpoint where the vehicle is empty, so the driver can take a break without disrupting any passenger's trip. These breaks also serve a second purpose: when a service runs late, the break is shortened so that the vehicle can get back on time. Providing these breaks is a great logistical challenge on busy loops, like the circular rail lines in Berlin, Moscow, and Tokyo. In 2009, the London Underground broke apart its Circle Line, which used to run as a continuous loop, partly to eliminate these problems.

## LIFE AFTER LOOPS

Loops touch things deep in the human psyche. When community leaders are asked in a meeting to talk about their transit needs, it's not uncommon for one of them to say, usually with circular hand gestures, that they need some kind of loop. The same people may use the word *linear* to mean narrow-minded or conceptually trapped. Straight lines can seem aggressive, whereas loops offer a sense of closure. They can even suggest the shape of an embrace.

If your agenda in life is to enjoy every moment and never worry about a destination, then the appeal of loops is undeniable. Tourist agencies, for example, often offer a very circuitous loop bus route whose purpose is to show you the whole city. Tourists are usually experience oriented rather than destination oriented, so loops can work well for their specialized needs.

But however much we may savor every moment of life, most of us still have jobs and families, so sometimes we just need to get there. We are at point A and need to be at point B as soon as possible. The shape of that desire is not a loop. It's a straight line.

# 5

# TOUCHING THE CITY: STOPS AND STATIONS

Transit serves the community at its stops or stations, which can be any thing from a massive railway terminal to an unmarked patch of dirt. We speak of "stations" for more substantial stops, especially stops served by fast services that are useful for longer trips. But all stations are stops, so for simplicity, I'll refer to them all as "stops."

High-ridership transit can't stop everywhere. Physically, it may be possible to stop anywhere along a line, and some low-ridership bus services do offer to stop in any safe location, a practice called "flag stops." But as ridership rises, this practice becomes less practical. Stopping consumes time, so we don't want to make two stops, very close together, just because two people weren't motivated to walk to the same stop.

In dense urban areas, any desire to attract riders, improve travel times, run efficiently, or compete with the private car will require transit agencies to push stops as far apart as possible while still serving the community. People get angry about that, so it's important to understand why the issue is unavoidable.

## COVERAGE OF A STOP

We usually visualize the area served by a stop as a circle around the stop (figure 5-1). There's a small ring defining the area from which you can walk

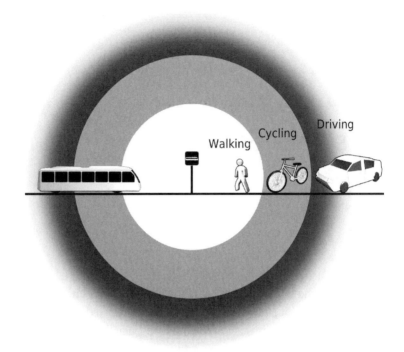

**Figure 5-1** Access radii from a stop. *Credit:* Erin Walsh

to the stop. A larger ring is the area from which you can cycle. A much larger area can reach the stop by car, in one of two modes:

- Park-and-ride, which means driving your car to the transit stop and parking it there.
- Dropoff, or what Americans sometimes call "Kiss-and-Ride," which means being driven to the stop by someone else (a relative, a friend, a caretaker) who will then drive away.

Dropoff is easy to accommodate because it doesn't take much space. Park-and-ride demands large quantities of space at a station.

The park-and-ride ring isn't a perfect circle like the others are. Motorists have considerable freedom to go to whatever park-and-ride location is convenient for them. In general, they tend to resist driving out of their intended direction of travel, so the park-and-ride catchment of a stop is usually defined by a large area that is upstream of the stop, where downstream is the traveler's intended direction.[1]

But while there are many ways to get to a transit stop, we plan for one method above all: walking. Sooner or later, everyone is a pedestrian. You may arrive at a stop by connecting transit service or by car or by bike, but unless you take your bike onboard, you'll still be a pedestrian at your destination.[a] So except at suburban stations that may be designed purely for park-and-ride, transit planners care most about walking.

Every stop or station has a walk radius, the area from which most people would be willing to walk to a stop. In the most idealized world, this radius defines a circle around each stop.

How big is the walk radius? Different people are comfortable walking different distances, so a truer view of these circles would be very fuzzy, gradually dissipating farther out from the stop. It's hard to draw that, though, and harder still to do calculations with it, so transit planners generally observe that the walking distance that most people seem to tolerate—the one beyond which ridership falls off dramatically—is about a quarter mile (400 m) for a local-stop service, but farther for a faster service.[2]

Of course, the circle is what the walk radius would be if you could walk absolutely anywhere in the area, including diagonally, through buildings and so forth. In the real world, we walk along a network of streets and paths. The design of that network is therefore a crucial element of walking distance, which means that it's also relevant to stop spacing. Consider the two drawings in figure 5-2.[3]

Your city probably contains examples of both types of street network. The car-oriented network on the left is full of obstacles to the pedestrian, so the actual area you can walk to (black) is less than a third of the ideal radius (gray). On the other hand, a dense grid of pedestrian links, like the one on the right, maximizes the possible walking distance. The actual area within walking distance is diamond shape—that is, a square rotated 45 degrees from the transit line. Almost two-thirds of the ideal radius is in walking distance in such a network.

Note how these things are connected in chains. Street network determines walking distance. Walking distance determines, in part, how

---

[a] The exception is a bicycle that can be folded, taken aboard unfolded, or placed on a rack on the exterior of a bus. These are very popular but tend to encounter limits of capacity in bigger, more crowded transit systems.

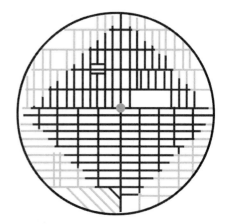

**Figure 5-2** Circular radius of a bus stop. Only the black segments are actually within walking distance. *Source:* Graphic by Urban Design 4 Health

far apart the stops can be. Stop spacing determines operating speed. So yes, the nature of the local street network affects how fast the transit line can run!

How do we decide about spacing? Consider the diamond-shaped catchment that's made possible by a fine street grid (figure 5-3).

Ideal stop spacing is as far apart as possible for the sake of speed, but people around the line have to be able to get to it. In particular, we're watching two areas of impact.

First, the *duplicate coverage area* is the area that has more than one stop within walking distance. In most situations, on flat terrain, you need to be able to walk to one stop, but not two, so duplicate coverage is a waste. Moving stops farther apart reduces the duplicate coverage area, which means that a greater number of unique people and areas are served by the stops.

Second, the *coverage gap* is the area that is within walking distance of the line but not of a stop. As we move stops farther apart, the coverage gap grows.

We would like to minimize both of these things, but in fact we have to choose between them. Close stop spacing means smaller coverage gaps but larger duplicate coverage area. Wide stop spacing means the opposite.

Which is worse: creating duplicate coverage area or leaving a coverage gap? It depends on whether your transit system is designed mainly to meet

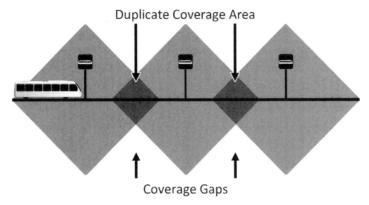

**Figure 5-3** Coverage gaps and duplicate coverage areas, assuming a fine pedestrian grid. *Credit:* Erin Walsh

the needs of transit-dependent persons or to compete for high ridership (a plumber's question that we'll explore more fully in chapter 10). If you care mostly about offering basic mobility to transit-dependent persons, you'll minimize the coverage gap so that everyone has access, and you won't care that much if the resulting line is slower and therefore less useful to other riders. On the other hand, if you want to maximize ridership, you'll worry more about the duplicate coverage area, because closer stop spacing means slower operations, which are both more expensive to operate and less useful to riders. So you'll tend to want to push stops farther apart.

A slope might shift the calculation.[4] Walking downhill is usually easier than walking uphill, so if a transit line is climbing or descending, some people will value having two stops so that they can walk downhill to one to depart, and walk downhill from the other one as they're returning.

Finally, although I've been talking about local stop service with a walk distance of about one quarter mile (400 m), the calculation is exactly the same for any distance. For example, if we are placing rapid transit stops and we think that the maximum walk distance to them is about 0.6 mile (1,000 m), we can set the stops 0.6 mile apart and end up with a duplicate coverage area that's the same size as the coverage gap. Then we can argue about whether, in the given situation, we should push wider or narrower, depending on what kind of development is in each area or gap. When transit is running on busy streets, we also have to adjust stop locations so that people can cross the street safely at every stop.

What is the ideal stop spacing then? It depends. The European HiTrans guides suggest that a spacing of 0.4 mile (600 m) "looks sensible" for local stops in continuously developed areas.[5] Actual European practice is usually in the range of 0.12 to 0.25 mile (200 to 400 m) for locally oriented services, but wider where demand is higher. (If demand is low, you can place closely spaced stops knowing that the bus usually won't have to stop at all of them; as ridership increases, however, the need for fewer, more widely spaced stops become more urgent.) North American habit is typically to put local stops even closer together, but some big-city agencies are now questioning this practice and trying to set stops a bit farther apart, at least on high-frequency, high-ridership lines where stop spacing is most critical to travel time. Again, all this matters most in busy areas where a transit vehicle is likely to have to stop at every stop.

## EXPRESS, RAPID, OR LOCAL?

In most transit systems, bus or rail, stop spacing tends to fall into one of the three categories shown in figure 5-4. No authority polices the definitions for these categories, and some agencies (including the New York City subways) use the word *express* for what I would call "rapid service." But the distinction is important, and we need words to describe it, so in this book I will use *local*, *rapid*, and *express* with these meanings:

- *Local* means serving closely spaced stops such that all points on or near the line are within walking distance of a stop.
- *Rapid* means regularly but widely spaced stops, usually every half mile (800 m) or more. Rapid spacing generally serves a series of areas around the stations rather than a continuous area along the whole line. There are many variations in rapid stop spacing, but it usually has this feature.
- *Express*, as I use the word in this book, means serving a long nonstop segment.[b] Typical express service is focused on a single major destina-

---

[b] The term *express*, in particular, is prone to a more vague meaning of "faster than local service." The US *Transit Capacity and Quality of Service Manual*, for example, defines express service as "service that has fewer stops and higher operating speed than regular service" (8-37). This vague use of *express* obscures the profound difference between all-

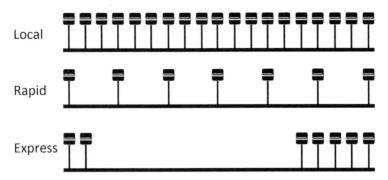

**Figure 5-4**  Three basic kinds of stopping pattern. *Credit:* Erin Walsh

tion, such as a downtown. It runs nonstop between that destination and the area it serves but makes numerous stops, spaced like a rapid or local, within that area. Commuter express buses and commuter rail are often express in this sense. Express service is inherently specialized, so it is frequently offered only during the peak commute period.

In North America, the term *rapid* may make you think of rail transit services, and *local* sounds like something buses do, but in fact bus and rail technologies can both do local or rapid service. Table 5-1, for example, shows some terms typically used to describe rail or bus in their various roles.

Rail transit includes not just the high-capacity rapid transit of big-city subways, for example, but also the streetcar or tram, which may run in local-stop mode just like a local bus.[6] Buses can be local, but they can also be rapid. When they are the latter, they're called limited-stop or rapid bus or Bus Rapid Transit.

When capitalized, the term *Rapid* increasingly means "not just rapid stop spacing, but also high all-day frequency," a meaning drawn from the term *rapid transit*.[7] The word *Rapid*, capitalized, is often used as a brand in North America, especially for services that provide rapid transit with buses.

*Limited-stop* or just *limited* is an old-fashioned term, originally from rail but now used heavily for buses, that means rapid stop spacing, but not

---

day, two-way services (which I'll call "limited" or "rapid") and the typical "commuter express" bus or train. Still, you will hear term *express* in many contexts where it means nothing more than "relatively fast."

**Table 5-1**  Stopping Patterns, Rail versus Bus

|  | Rapid (faster, fewer stops) | Local (slower, more stops) | Express (a long nonstop segment) |
|---|---|---|---|
| Rail | Subway, "Metro," some commuter rail and light rail | Tram, streetcar | Some commuter rail |
| Bus | "Bus Rapid Transit," "Rapid Bus," "limited-stop bus" | Typical local bus | Commuter express bus (e.g., on freeway) |

necessarily a long span or high frequency. In Los Angeles, for example, a service that runs a high frequency all day with rapid stop spacing is called a "Metro Rapid," while a service that runs rapid stop spacing but with less frequency, or only during the peak, is called a "limited".

Bus operators are used to people carelessly boarding limited buses when they want the local and then getting angry when the bus doesn't let them off at their stop. The word *limited* has thus evolved as a warning word, trying to prevent this mistake. Of course, this has the unfortunate effect of accentuating the negative ("may not stop where you want") instead of the positive ("runs faster than a local").

## THE RAPID REVOLUTION

Transit systems that have a social service history have typically focused on local service—often with very close stop spacing—because easy access to the service was presumed to be more important than speed. The North American tendency with heavy urban bus lines has been to run local service all the time as frequently as possible, and to add limited-stop service only when and where there is a surge of demand. For example, it's normal to see an urban bus route with frequent local service all day and limited-stop service just during the peak commute period.

In the past ten years, however, there's been a dramatic shift toward all-day frequent Rapid bus services, bus lines that run in rapid mode at high frequency for a long service day. Usually, a local runs alongside them on the same street, making local stops for people who can't or don't want to walk to the Rapid. North American leaders in this area include Vancouver's B-Line product and the Los Angeles Metro Rapid network, both of which are now more than a decade old.

Los Angeles is a city of such vast distances that it's a good place to see the value of Rapid buses. The city has long had an intensive bus system, and of course it once had a large streetcar network, but its current rail rapid transit system dates from only 1990. Even after the next thirty years' worth of rail transit plans are built, most of Los Angeles will still not be within walking distance of a rail station.

Faced with this reality, and also with the long distances that people must travel in the city, the transit agency developed the Metro Rapid product, which consists of distinctive red buses running long lines across Los Angeles in a rough grid pattern, stopping only every half mile (800 m) or so. They run all day, usually at frequencies of 15 minutes or better. Within the city limits of Los Angeles, they also get priority at many traffic signals. They are not in exclusive lanes, as this was politically impossible at the time. Now, however, such lanes are planned, created mostly by removing on-street parking, on the busiest of the Rapid corridors, Wilshire Boulevard.[8]

The Los Angeles transit agency still also runs "local" buses, and on streets with no Rapid there may still be "limited-stop" service. But on Wilshire, their busiest corridor, the Rapids have upended the traditional notion that local service is the basic product.

Between downtown and Westwood, the Wilshire Rapid runs every 6 to 8 minutes all day while the local comes every 11 minutes. The Rapid is around 25 percent faster. Ridership is high on both services, but 51 percent of all Wilshire riders are on the Rapid. Average trip lengths are 2.7 miles (4.3 km) on the local and 5.9 miles (9.4 km) on the Rapid. Weekday productivity on the Rapid is over 60 boardings per hour, which means that on average, one person boards for every minute a bus is operating. This is stellar performance for such a long line.[9]

On Wilshire, the Rapid has been a success, even lacking bus lanes and competing with a fragmentary subway line that duplicates it over the densest 3 miles (5 km) approaching downtown. Most Los Angeles corridors have much less frequency, and less density, so the performance of the Rapids is lower, but Wilshire is a one possible model for a boulevard of the future. Already lined with several patches of towers and anchored by the high-rise centers of downtown in the east and Westwood/UCLA in the west, Wilshire is an ideal transit market. If Los Angeles continues to grow denser, other boulevards will acquire similar features and be ready to support successful Rapids, especially if this possibility is considered as the city's growth is being planned. (We'll return to the challenge of boulevard transit in chapter 15.)

So in big cities with long travel corridors, the Metro Rapid forces us to question tradition. Why, exactly, do we think of the local-stop bus as the basic product, and of "limited-stop" or Rapid service as something we add only as demand requires? What if we did the opposite?

Imagine, for a moment, an alternate vision of transit in which the first priority was to move people quickly over longer distances, with a product that stopped only every half mile (800 m) or more but that was fast enough to be worth walking to? Local services attract most of their riders from a quarter-mile (400 m) radius, but people often walk farther to get to a Rapid stop. If we made that the standard, then in a grid of arterials half a mile apart, everyone is within acceptable walking distance of a Rapid stop (figure 5-5). Such a product would assume that the communities it serves are walkable, and would aim to complement walking rather than competing with it.

If that were the vision, the Rapid would be the primary product, and the locals would be secondary; in some areas you might not need them at all. And whenever you can combine all the services on a street into a single stopping pattern, you can *dramatically* improve the frequency, thus cutting waiting time.[10]

But of course, not everyone can walk a half mile (800 m), or is willing to in all situations, and some service areas have street patterns or urban designs that make walking more difficult, so there's a market for local-stop services. Some seniors and disabled persons are not able to walk half a mile to access their only transit service, but can tolerate lower frequencies on a more specialized small bus that serves their needs.

In commercial districts, there's often a market for a local shuttle that stops often, so that you can just hop on if you see it coming. In Los Angeles, for example, short shuttle trips within commercial districts are usually the work of separate routes. These may share a Rapid's street for a short distance but stop more often.

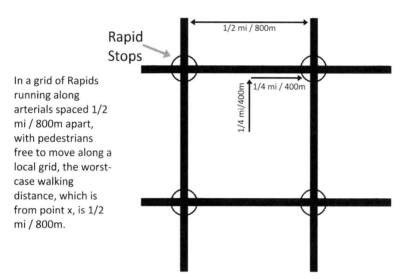

In a grid of Rapids running along arterials spaced 1/2 mi / 800m apart, with pedestrians free to move along a local grid, the worst-case walking distance, which is from point x, is 1/2 mi / 800m.

**Figure 5-5** Maximum walk distances for Rapid spacing. *Credit:* Erin Walsh

Still, the question arises: If there's frequent, all-day Rapid service running the length of a long and busy boulevard, stopping at least every 0.5 mile (800 meters), how much local service do you need, and what kind? If a boulevard is, say, 20 miles (32 km) long and you have a Rapid covering that distance, do you really need a single continuous local? Perhaps what you need are frequent local shuttles in the commercial districts and then longer, less-frequent locals that provide basic access along the other segments but that may not need to run frequently or cost much..

On the other hand, if you set your spacing at one quarter mile (400 m), could you still maintain the Rapid's speed using other improvements that are increasingly common on Rapid bus service, such as off-board fare collection? If so, perhaps this spacing (a common European spacing for frequent *local* service) could be the standard that would allow us to combine Rapids and locals into a single product that's still fast enough to serve long-distance needs. Bus lanes (to which we'll return in chapter 8) could also be a crucial part of a package that makes a wider stop spacing acceptable.

Few transit agencies are thinking this radically today, partly because most are evolving from a tradition in which slow locals were considered the default form of service. Still, the obvious attraction of Rapid bus services, and their ability to improve travel time for large numbers of people, requires us to broaden our notions of what an ideal or "normal" spacing would be. New information tools may also change our experience of walking and waiting. Will we be more tolerant of longer walks if we are sure we won't have to wait at the stop? In cities that already offer real-time information about the actual location of a bus or railcar, my walk to the stop is more pleasant because I'm not anxious about whether I might miss it. Could this information, readily available to everyone by phone, help us tolerate walking farther, thus supporting wider stop spacing that would in turn yield faster service?

The question of how to balance local with Rapid service is tied to a big question that will dominate chapter 10: ridership or coverage? Are you designing our transit system mainly for high ridership, with the environmental and fare revenue benefits of that? Or, are you running a social service designed to help smaller numbers of people with limited ability or willingness to walk? If the latter, clearly you'll run a network of slow local services that are easy to walk to. But if ridership is the goal, and your trip distances are long, you'll run as much Rapid service as you can, with a stop spacing calculated to optimize total trip times (including walking, waiting, and riding) overall.

The balance of Rapid versus local service also affects sustainability goals. When you run heavy local service stopping every two blocks, achieving an average speed of 12 miles (19 km) per hour or less, what are you competing with? Such slow services are perhaps three times your walking speed, but is this enough of an advantage for the service to be worth waiting for, or is it better to just start walking?

Obviously, it depends on how far you're going. Rapid service can average more than 20 miles (32 km) per hour on a busy street, and much faster if it has an exclusive lane. That's a speed where transit can compete with the car for many trips, especially if there's also a disincentive to driving, such as parking cost and hassle.

So it comes down to this: *The faster transit runs, the more it competes with cars. The slower it runs, the more it competes with walking.* Which competition is more urgent? Well, we need to serve people with limited ability to walk. But we also have an environmental and urban livability agenda that requires us to compete with cars.

This isn't a proposal, but it is a line of thought that agencies should be exploring. How little local service do we need if we have really good Rapid service? Do we need local service on every segment of a Rapid, or just on certain segments with high senior/disabled needs or commercial districts? Can we create strong Rapids by simply shifting resources from existing locals? Or can a compromise stop spacing—say 400 m—allow us to combine Rapid and local into one very frequent service? Many cities are thinking about this. Los Angeles alone provides enough experience to help you argue all sides of the question, and find your own view.

## LINE SPACING IS STOP SPACING

Finally, the geometry that governs stop spacing also governs the spacing of parallel lines. In the Los Angeles example, the half-mile (800 m) spacing of parallel lines ensures that the quarter-mile (400 m) walk radius from one line doesn't overlap the walk radius of the other. If it does, you're providing duplicate service to the same people, which is always less useful than providing unique service for different people.

One of the most common mistakes in transit planning is to invent a new line, in response to some political initiative, without thinking about how it affects the existing lines that it may overlap. Overlaying new lines on top of existing ones is politically easy, but by creating duplicate coverage, it often leads to a less efficient network overall.

# 6

# PEAK OR ALL DAY?

If you live in a large house in a low-density suburb and usually get around by car, you may not think much about transit until you confront the problem of congestion. And since congestion first becomes a problem during the *peak commute period*, also known as "rush hour," you may start out caring only about transit that runs at that time. Perhaps you support transit in hopes that it will make other people leave their cars at home, so that there's more space on the road for yours. Or, perhaps you want an alternative to the congested freeway for your own daily commute and have looked at whether your transit system provides one.

If this is your reality, then your interest in transit may be mostly in peak services. In this case, you may take a passing interest in midday, evening, and weekend service, but you'll probably have two reasons for doing so.

First, you may know that you don't always control when you can leave work, so it's easier to commute on transit if you know that there's some midday and evening service so that you can come home early or late if you need to.

Second, you may be aware that some people need to get around at all hours, and you may feel comfortable supporting a basic service for them. Someone has to work at McDonald's, after all. The people in these low-wage jobs may not be able to own cars, and they often work shifts that begin and end outside the usual peak period. You may also have teenage children or elderly relatives who don't want to be dependent on you for transportation, and midday and evening service can meet those basic needs. But if these are your only reasons to support all-day and evening service, you probably have only an indirect interest in how well that service functions and how useful it is.

If this sketch describes you, then you form the dominant constituency of transit in many suburban areas. So your transit system will do its best to meet your needs as a peak commuter, typically by designing specialized services to make your commute easier. Most low-density suburban areas in North America have service that runs only, or at least mainly, during the peak commute period. These include express buses, commuter rail lines, and shuttles between rail stations and suburban business parks. Some waterfront cities have peak-only commuter ferries.

## PEAKING: HOW AND WHY IT HAPPENS

Transit planners say a network is *peaked* if it carries far more riders during the peak commute period than it does in the midday, evening, and week-end periods. The most peaked systems are almost always those devoted to lower-density suburban areas, where driving all day is easy and only the peak commute motivates most people to try transit. The simple graphs in figure 6-1, from the Portland transit agency TriMet, show typical peaking patterns for several basic kinds of service.

Line 45 (figure 6-1a) serves low-density suburbs in Portland's south-west, connecting them to downtown. In this suburban-dominated market, peaking is extreme. The busiest peak hours are more than three times as busy as the midday.

Line 15 (figure 6-1b) is a typical inner-city line, devoted to short trips within the densest part of the city, including downtown. Here, the peak is barely twice as high as the midday.

Line 72 (figure 6-1c) is a crosstown line; it doesn't go to downtown but crosses many lines that do. It runs frequently along busy commercial boulevards with moderate-density, typically car-oriented retail strips with some apartments behind them. The first impression from Line 72 is the high afternoon peak at 15:00 (3:00 p.m.) corresponding to when schools let out. This is a common pattern on transit systems that also do school transportation; the afternoon school peak is higher than the morning one because many parents drop their children at school on the way to work but cannot be there to pick them up.

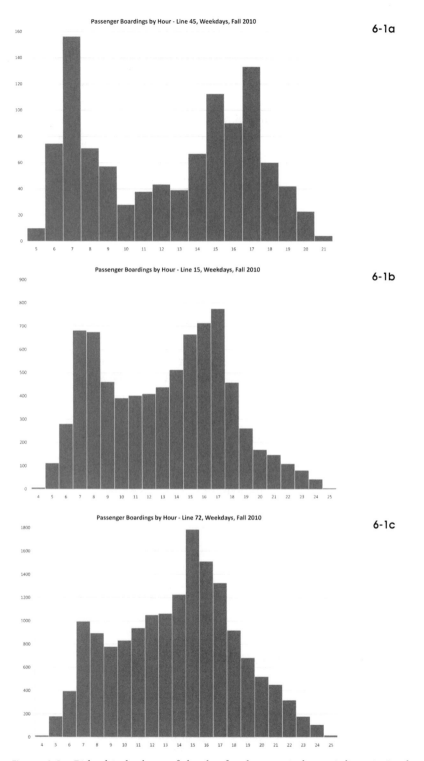

**Figure 6-1**   Ridership by hour of the day for three typical transit lines in Portland.
*Source:* TriMet

Many people also use Line 72 to commute in various directions, but it doesn't have a one-way high-volume commute, such as radial lines have into downtown. So apart from its high school peak in the late afternoon, Line 72's demand is relatively flat across the daylight hours of the day. This is the most efficient situation for transit, because it means that a consistent pattern of service can be run all day. That's why Line 72 has long been one of Portland's most productive, in terms of riders per unit of service provided.

We can observe two important things here. First, services that don't go into a major downtown, and that serve a diffuse mixture of trip patterns, can have remarkably little peaking. Apart from the impact of the afternoon school peak, people ride these lines in rather even volumes in both directions all day.

Second, lines linking downtown to lower-density outer suburbs, like Line 45, are generally the most peaked.

Dense cities, such as the inner-city area served by Portland's Line 15, also show a much stronger market for transit that runs all day, evening, and weekend. The density and diversity of core cities make them easy places to live without a car, or with two or more adults sharing a car. This means, in turn, that people tend to rely on transit for a range of all-day travel needs, not just the commute. Of course, transit also serves many jobs, such as in restaurants, where shifts tend to begin and end during the midday or evening period, not right on the standard commute peak.

In using these Portland examples, I've referred to downtown as though it's the main transit destination. Portland has a relatively strong downtown, but other cities are different and will show different peaking effects as a result. Los Angeles, for example, has several high-rise employment and activity centers that each function like a downtown, and service into any of them will show these same patterns.

## TWO WAYS TO THINK ABOUT PEAKS

Your transit demand, whatever it is, probably shows some degree of peaking. Given this, you can think about your demand in two ways, which will lead to completely different designs for your network (figure 6-2).

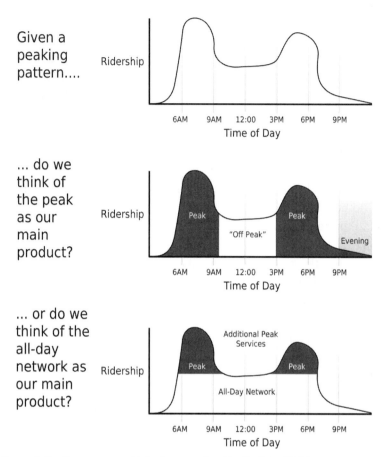

**Figure 6-2** Two ways to think about peaks. *Credit:* Erin Walsh

- *Peak-first.* You can think of the peak service as your most fundamental product and of the other times of day as a secondary or supplemental product. When you hear someone refer to the midday as the "off-peak," as though it's inferior or secondary to the peak, they are suggesting at least a hint of this view.
- *Base-first.* You can think of the pattern of service that runs all the time as your most fundamental product and of the service added on the peak as your supplemental product.

If your peaks are very high and your midday demand is very low, as in most low-density suburban areas, it will seem natural to think peak-first. If you're in an inner city, with a high all-day demand and modest additional peaks, it will seem natural to think base-first. But this is one of those questions that's often answered subconsciously, without really thinking about it.

Many transportation planners are trained in the work of evaluating possible physical improvements, such as new or expanded roads or transit lines. This process—including conceptualization, design, and estimation of expected usage—tends to be peak-first. Classic highway engineering, for example, designs a road to handle the traffic that it will carry on the peak and isn't bothered by the fact that these roads will be relatively empty for the other 20 or more hours of the day.

If you carry that view into transit planning, you'll design services and infrastructure for the peak as well. You'll create commuter rail lines or express buses and will usually organize them around park-and-rides in suburban areas. But unlike the road planner, the transit planner has a problem with the midday, evening, and weekend periods. What kind of service should we run then? And if the infrastructure and institutions are designed based *solely* on peak-first thinking, they may not provide any good options for serving those times.

Commuter rail lines focused on North American suburbs offer an especially vivid example of the trade-offs involved in peak-first planning. The typical North American commuter rail line has relatively high operating costs per train, because there are usually several employees onboard. There are one or two people in the cab plus one or more "conductors" (the title may vary) who move through the train checking fares. The high cost of running each train can make sense during the peak when the trains are crowded, but the rest of the time, the decision about whether to run at all can be hard. Somebody has to drive the train, and somebody has to check fares, so you need several employees for each train, even on midday trains that won't be crowded.

So when demand drops in the midday, commuter rail can adjust only by running fewer trains—in other words, a poor frequency—or shutting down entirely. (Commuter rail often shares tracks with freight, which can be another obstacle to frequency.) And as we'll see in chapter 12, low frequency doesn't just mean less chance of running when a customer needs it; it also means poor connections with other transit services, making it hard to complete trips to anywhere that isn't right on the rail line. The cost structure of commuter rail simply forbids abundant all-day operations, because commuter rail's high labor cost only works when the trains are crowded. In other words, *commuter rail is intrinsically a peak-first concept.*

Sometimes, commuter rail is established in a corridor where the market could support efficient two-way, all-day frequent rapid transit. Once that happens, the commuter rail service can be an obstacle to any further improvement. The commuter rail creates a line on the map, so many decision makers assume that the needs are met, and may not understand that the line's poor frequency outside the peak prevents it from functioning as rapid transit. At the same time, efforts to convert commuter rail operations to all-day high-frequency service (which requires enough automation to reduce the number of employees per train to one, if not zero) founder against institutional resistance, especially within labor unions. (Such a change wouldn't necessarily eliminate jobs overall, but it would turn all the jobs into train-driver jobs, running more trains.)

This problem has existed for decades, for example, around the Caltrain commuter rail line between San Francisco and San Jose. This corridor has the perfect geography for all-day frequent rapid transit: super-dense San Francisco at one end, San Jose at the other, and a rail that goes right through the downtowns of almost all the suburban cities in between. In fact, the downtowns are where they are because they grew around the rail line, so the fit between the transit and urban form could not be more perfect. Not far off the line, easily served by shuttles, are all the major employers of Silicon Valley (including the headquarters of Google, Apple, Facebook, and Hewlett Packard), not to mention Stanford University. If you look at the amount of development that's within walking distance of stations, the Caltrain corridor far exceeds most of the suburban areas where BART (Bay Area Rapid Transit) operates all-day frequent rapid transit.

Caltrain, however, has a long history of operation with labor-intensive and therefore infrequent commuter rail. The midday service is hourly at this writing, which is useless for the spontaneous trips that true rapid transit would allow. Because Caltrain is so much less frequent than its market requires, there has to be an overlapping network of buses running along the same path. Scheduling local connecting buses to meet the train is hard to do outside the peak, because the train is often less frequent than the buses. The result is inefficiency for transit agencies and frustration for their potential passengers. Caltrain achieves unusually high farebox return (percentage of operating cost paid by fares) because it runs mostly when it's busy, but its presence is also a source of confusion: the line on the map gives the appearance that this corridor has rapid transit service, but in fact Caltrain is of limited use outside the commute hour.

## THE COSTS OF PEAK-ONLY SERVICE

Three major cost-effectiveness barriers face a transit agency that focuses on peak-only service, such as commuter express runs (bus or rail) into a typical downtown. They are (1) the need for many driver shifts to end where they began, (2) reasonable limits on how peak shifts can be scheduled, and (3) the need to own a fleet that's used for only a few hours a day.

### Labor Costs

First, in most transit operations, drivers and any other onboard staff generally expect to end their shifts where they began. A bus or train may look impressively crowded in the peak direction, but the true cost of operations is based on the labor shift, and the staff on those buses and trains must usually be paid to travel back to their point of origin, either by driving their transit vehicle or by riding another train, bus, or van.[a] So the labor time used by the one-way peak commute run is sometimes less than half of the total for which the staff must be paid.

Labor contracts also frequently specify a minimum shift time, such as 4 hours for a part-time shift. This requirement is understandable from the driver's viewpoint; it's silly to commute just to do 2 hours of paid work. But because of these provisions, short pieces of peak-only work often cost even more because drivers must be paid these minimums.

In the early 1980s, when I was an undergraduate intern in the planning department of Portland's TriMet, I remember a day when the manager of scheduling was tearing his hair out in frustration. The agency faced budget cuts and was having to cut service, but the general manager (the chief executive officer of the agency) had instructed them to cut only out-

---

[a] Regardless of where the trip starts, a driver must be paid for an out-of-service trip in the reverse peak direction to return to the shift's starting point. This can be either before or after the in-service trip.

side the peak. "Don't cut the peak," he had said. "The peak is our bread and butter!"

But as it turned out, there was no way to protect the peak service from cuts and still save any money. They could cut midday service, but this would turn all-day shifts into peak-only shifts, which would make those shifts more expensive to run. This effect was so pronounced that it canceled out most of the cost savings from the service cut.

An all-day service pattern is usually made up of full-time shifts, generally around 7 to 8 hours long. For example, many transit services run for a 16-hour day—say, 5:00 a.m. to 9:00 p.m.—which comes apart nicely into two full-time 8-hour shifts. Both drivers and transit managers usually prefer these shifts, because they use staff time efficiently.

Peak-only service, by contrast, usually requires either part-time staff—who work only in the morning or only in the afternoon—or else full-time staff working *split shifts*, shifts that have two pieces of work with time off between them. Some drivers like split shifts, but if you're raising a family, they can be the job from hell. Perhaps you go to work at 4:30 a.m. and get off at 8:30 a.m. You have the day free. Then you go back to work at, say, 3:30 p.m. and get off at 6:30 p.m. If your commute is a half hour, you get home at 7:00 p.m. and must leave for work at 4:00 the next morning, *only 9 hours later*. If your family members are at work or school during the day, you basically never see them awake, except on weekends. In agencies that allocate work by seniority, these shifts are so undesirable that they tend to go to the most junior staff, even though these are the employees most likely to have young children.

Labor contracts vary dramatically from one agency to another, but this fact of life doesn't: the split shifts required for peak-only service are very tough on employees. Staff understandably insist on being paid more for working them, through various "penalty rates" (surcharges on the usual hourly pay rate) or other restrictions on scheduling. For example, a typical contract provision on split shifts will restrict the "spread," which is the duration from the beginning of the morning piece of work to the end of the evening piece. These reasonable requirements are part of the higher cost of peak-only service.

Part-time staff are an increasingly common solution; some people can fit a 4-hour shift of driving into a life that includes another career or full-time study. But even in that case, the short shift is inefficient, due to the minimum block of the time that a driver must be paid for, even if he's needed for less than that.

Another option that may deserve more exploration, though labor unions will resist it, is *worker-driver service*. A worker-driver is a commuter who is hired by the transit agency to drive a transit route that matches his own commute and keeps the bus near his home overnight or collects it in the morning from an operating base nearby. The worker-driver then drives a scheduled commuter route to the workplace in the morning and drives a similar route back in the evening, carrying passengers and charging fares just as any bus would do. In Kitsap and Mason Counties, Washington, this method has long been used for commutes to military bases, and gradually it's been expanded to civilians.[1] Some private commuter service operators also use the technique. Worker-driver services present many challenges, and they won't work in most big-city settings, but they solve the big problem of one-way commuter service: the need for a professional driver who usually must (a) be paid to return to his point of origin and (b) be paid extra for the inconvenience of a short or split shift.

## Fleet Costs

Finally, of course, a transit agency bears a large cost tied to the size of the fleet it must own. Fleet size depends on how many vehicles you need at once, and that, of course, depends on your peak service, not your all-day pattern. Many transit agencies must purchase, license, store, and maintain a vehicle that makes only one round trip per day. That's a huge inefficiency compared to an all-day operation whose fleet may work 10 to 20 hours each day.

Every transit agency gets complaints from people who saw a bus, train, or ferry running empty or nearly empty, because it looks like a waste of resources. Usually it isn't, especially if you see such a vehicle outside the peak period, when demand is lower, or traveling against the peak direction (away from your downtown in the morning or into it in the afternoon) or near the end of a line. It's normal for loads to be low in these situations, even on very successful services.[b]

---

[b] Because operating cost (especially for buses) is mostly labor, a big bus carrying a few people isn't much more expensive to run than a small bus, on which the same people would be a full load. Small buses use less fuel, but this is a small part of the cost, so it's never

But if you see a transit vehicle running nearly empty during the peak period and in the peak commute direction, you may be seeing some actual waste. Suppose that a commuter express bus, doing a long run from a distant suburb into the city, carries only fifteen people, less than half a seated load. If the transit agency is looking at its cost-effectiveness fairly, this situation should look much, much worse than a bus with fifteen people at noon, running on an all-day, two-way line. For this one commuter express run, the agency has spent hundreds of thousands of dollars to buy the bus, thousands more for the land on which to store it, and thousands per year to maintain and operate it, including penalty rates for the driver who works a brutal schedule and is kept from spending time with family most days—all to serve only fifteen people!

Deleting that service, moreover, might not leave those fifteen people stranded. In many cases, they might still have a local bus connection to some other express line. They will complain about having to make a connection, and may even threaten to stop riding. But even if fifteen people stop riding and you can redeploy that bus to an area where it will run full or be useful for a longer period, you may (depending on your goals) come out ahead.

There's nothing wrong with running peak-only service if you understand the real cost. Still, transit agencies should monitor the cost of running peak-only rather than all-day, and the ridership that results, so that they can be sure that the investment makes sense and see whether there are ways to economize. In some cases, it may be possible to expand peak service into all-day service with a relatively small increment of cost. Midday and evening service can even attract more peak commuters, because it provides a "guaranteed ride home" for commuters who unexpectedly need to leave work early or stay late.

## THE PLUMBER'S QUESTION: PEAK OR ALL DAY? PEAK COMMUTERS OR EVERYONE?

So the plumber's question about peaks, a crucial question with no factual answer, is the one presented by the graphics earlier in this chapter:

---

worthwhile to switch out a large bus for a small one to avoid running a big bus when demand is low, given the labor cost of driving the bus back to the base to exchange it.

- Are you a peak transit commute agency that maybe runs some midday and evening service on the side ("peak-first")?
- Or, are you an all-day transit agency, one that aspires to be useful for many purposes across the day and evening but that may supplement your service during the peak period to handle the higher demand then ("base-first")?

As a rule, peak-first thinking prevails at commuter rail and outer-suburban bus agencies, who typically serve areas that generate low demand outside the peaks. Agencies that think base-first tend to serve dense inner cities or university towns, both of which produce high demand all day, including evenings and weekends. You may also make the second choice if your agency's purpose is circulation *within* a small city or suburb, where you don't handle a major peak commute.

Obviously, the balance between peak and all-day service is a spectrum. Your agency may be at any point on a spectrum, from one that runs no midday service to one whose peak and midday service levels are identical. Your agency may also have goals about how much they focus on one market or the other, goals that have been arrived at through an honest discussion about the various options and their cost.

But in my experience, many agencies don't have this conversation, and can get stuck in habits that may not match changing priorities. If, for example, your city is developing more dense and mixed-use communities where many of the needs of life can be met without driving, it may be encouraging, consciously or not, lower rates of car ownership. Low-car or no-car lifestyles, in turn, mean that transit has to be available for many of life's purposes, not just the peak commute. If this is happening, the transit agency needs to focus on its midday, evening, and weekend offerings (which in the past may have been a social service for the "captive rider") so that it forms a consistent, reliable, and attractive product.

# 7

# FREQUENCY IS FREEDOM

In the conceptual diagram of our seven transit demands in chapter 2, one feature of transit should stand out. *Frequency* has a direct role in meeting four of the seven transit demands, more than any of the others. It also dominates three of the seven phases of a trip, and it's the main measure of everyone's least favorite phase: waiting. Frequency is also the essence of the distinction between routes (sites of occasional transportation events) and lines (transit that is there whenever you need it).

Closely related to frequency is the concept of *span*, which denotes the times of day when service begins and ends, on each day of the week. Services with a short span, such as the peak-only services we explored in chapter 6, are usually specialized around certain rider groups. Service that wants to be useful to everyone, and to function as part of a network, needs a long span, extending across the day and evening and also across the weekend. Some urban services, bus and rail, run continuously all day and night.

Frequency and span are the essence of freedom for a transit passenger. High-frequency, long-span service is there whenever you want to use it, even for spontaneous trips. If we want people to choose more transit-dependent lifestyles by owning fewer cars, they will need transit that's there most of the time, and where they'll never have to wait long. Both frequency and span are fundamental features of transit systems that feel empowering, such as subways you may have ridden in dense cities of Europe or East Asia, systems on which the whole city seems content to rely.

But frequency and span are expensive. Doubling frequency (that is, halving the headway, say, from 30 minutes to 15 minutes) doubles operating cost. Each increase in the length of the service day is also a corresponding increase in operating cost. So these investments are a high-stakes game, with high costs and high potential to transform the transit experience in a way that vastly expands its usefulness.

Yet frequency and span are also oddly invisible. Think about all of the ways that you may form ideas about a transit system, especially if you don't ride it yourself:

- You see maps of the network or of certain transit proposals.
- You read descriptions of transit proposals in the newspaper, often accompanied by maps, always emphasizing *where* the proposed service will operate.
- You see the transit vehicles moving around your city. You may also notice signage—on stops and transit vehicles—indicating where each service goes.
- You see people waiting at bus, rail, or ferry stops and may generalize about transit based on your impressions of those people.
- You see images of transit vehicles in film, television, and music video, often used in ways that encourage you to generalize about the quality of the service and the types of people who use it.

Those sources form powerful images that connect with people's existing ideas of their city. When we get the same impression from multiple sources, we tend to become more confident in it. So, all of these sources together can appear to form a firm basis for developing strong views about transit.

But *nothing in any of those impressions shows you the impact of frequency,* even though, as we've seen, frequency is the single most important variable in meeting our mobility desires. Nor do they give any signal about span. This conceptual invisibility of frequency and span may well be the single greatest barrier to coherent decision making about transit.

## DANGERS ON THE MAP

Of course, if you try to use transit yourself, you'll learn about frequency and span fast. To be useful, transit must exist in both space and time. It must run not just *where* we need it but also *when* we need it. Unless it does both, it doesn't exist for us at all.

The prevailing habit of most transit systems is to advertise *where* they go but treat *when* as though it were a detail. Many systems publish a map showing all of the lines they operate but giving no clear visual cue about whether these lines run every 5 minutes, or once an hour, or a few times during rush hour only, or once every Tuesday afternoon. To figure that out, you often have to choose a line and then explore its timetable, which requires you to wade through a great deal of detail just to get a basic sense of whether the service is there when you need it. The implication is that *when* the service runs—frequency and span—is just another detail.

Figure 7-1, for example, is a slice of the system map published by Seattle's main local transit agency, King County Metro Transit, in 2010.[1] This slice shows Queen Anne Hill, and surrounding neighborhoods, just northwest of downtown Seattle. In the original, the line and number bullets are all blue, but nothing is lost reproducing it in black and white, because there is no differentiation by color.

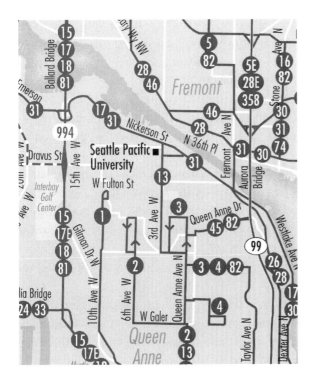

**Figure 7-1** Slice of King County Metro system map: Seattle's Queen Anne Hill in early 2011. *Source:* Map courtesy of King County Metro Transit, February 2011

The problem is that all of the bus lines on this map—both the graphic of the line and the line number bullet—look like the same kind of product. But, in fact:

- Some of these lines have frequent all-day service. On these lines, a bus is probably coming in the next few minutes at almost any time of day.
- Some of these lines have infrequent all-day service. You'll get a bus there, but you may wait a long time, and there may be no evening service.
- Some of these lines are peak-only. If it isn't rush hour and you aren't going in the peak commute direction, these lines don't exist for you.
- Two of these lines, the 81 and 82, are nighttime-only routes. They exist only when none of the others do, in the middle of the night. Although the map shows these services interacting with others, no such interaction ever occurs in reality.

These are matters not of service quality, but of service existence. They are questions about whether the service exists at all, for you, when you need it. So if your map's goal is information, as opposed to advertising, it makes little sense to think of them as details requiring complex investigations by the customer.

I do not mean to criticize King County Metro in particular, because the problem is commonplace in transit mapping. Most published transit maps, in many cities, still make no visual distinction among such basic differences of frequency and span.

If you look at almost any street map, a map designed for motorists or to give people a general sense of the shape of the city, you'll see clear signals that the lines on the map are not all equal. A Google street map, for example, uses simple line weight and color to visually distinguish three classes of road: freeways, arterial streets, and other, lesser streets. All map users rely on this hierarchy to organize their mental image of a city, regardless of their means of travel.

If a street map for a city showed every road with the same kind of line, so that a freeway looked just like a gravel road, we'd say it was a bad map. If we can't identify the major streets and freeways, we can't see the basic structure of the city, and without that, we can't really make use of the map's information. Which road should a motorist use when traveling a long distance across the city? Such a map wouldn't tell you, and without that, you couldn't really begin.

So, a transit map that makes all lines look equal is like a road map that doesn't show the difference between a freeway and a gravel road.

Now, you could argue that good road maps distinguish their lines based on implied differences in *speed*. We expect a freeway to be faster than a boulevard, and a boulevard to be faster than a local street, and that's why those types of road are distinguished on road maps. Should transit maps should be doing the same thing, distinguishing different types of line by their average speed?

Many transit agencies do exactly that. For example, they may have a separate category of "express" services that run part of the time on freeways. They may present these services as separate and in some way premium, highlighting them on their network maps, often in red.

But some of these express routes—which look like the most important routes on the agency's map—don't even run all day. A bright red line on the San Jose, California, transit map, for example, may mean just a few trips at rush hour, and in only one direction.[a] These red lines look like backbones of the network, but in fact they represent something that's usually not there.

Emphasizing *speed over frequency* can make sense in contexts where everyone is expected to plan around the timetable, including peak-only commute services and very long trips with low demand. In all other contexts, though, it seems to be a common motorist's error. Roads are there all the time, so their speed is the most important fact that distinguishes them. But transit is only there if it's coming soon. If you have a car, you can use a road whenever you want and experience its speed. But transit has to exist when you need it (span), and it needs to be coming soon (frequency). Otherwise, waiting time will wipe out any time savings from a faster service. Unless you're comfortable planning your life around a particular scheduled trip, speed is worthless without frequency, so a transit map that

---

[a] Santa Clara Valley Transportation Authority, "Bus and Rail Map," http://www.vta.org/schedules/schedules_bymap.html (accessed June 30, 2011). Again, no particular criticism of this agency is implied. Their map is just an especially clear example of a common industry practice.

screams about speed and whispers about frequency may simply be sowing confusion.

## FREQUENT NETWORK BRANDING: SELLING WHAT MATTERS

If you are thinking about the transit product from a marketing standpoint, emphasizing speed over frequency is understandable. Selling is about accentuating the positive, and if some lines are really infrequent, the marketing impulse will be to avoid calling attention to that.

But any attempt to conceal low frequencies also conceals high frequencies. If you're someone who doesn't like to wait, one encounter with an infrequent service can make you decide that *none* of your transit system's lines can be trusted to be there when you need them. And if your agency advertises the frequency of its rail lines but not the frequency of its buses, you may decide that buses are somehow intrinsically infrequent. So, it's quite understandable that if you don't like to wait, and don't have the time or inclination to wade through the detail of timetables, you'll decide that your transit system simply doesn't want you as a customer.

Since the late 1990s, some leading North American transit agencies (along with Adelaide in Australia and several on other continents) have been exploring ways to combat the invisibility of frequency and span. The key idea is to identify those parts of the network (bus, rail, or ferry) that run frequently enough, and for a long enough span, that you really can rely on them for most of the needs of daily life. Obviously, this impulse is most strongly felt in cities that really want to drive down car ownership by providing useful and liberating alternatives, and that see public transit as an important part of that mix.

Some transit agencies now have an explicit Frequent Network brand (local brand names vary) and publish maps showing only that network. Figure 7-2 is the map for Metro Transit in Minneapolis–St. Paul.[2] Note that it shows both light rail (Line 55) and frequent bus services. A separate map shows the entire transit network, but highlights the Frequent Network in yellow so that you can see both how it works and how it connects with other services.[3]

Think of this map as an answer to the following request: I'm someone who likes to use transit and would love to rely on it more, but I'm just too

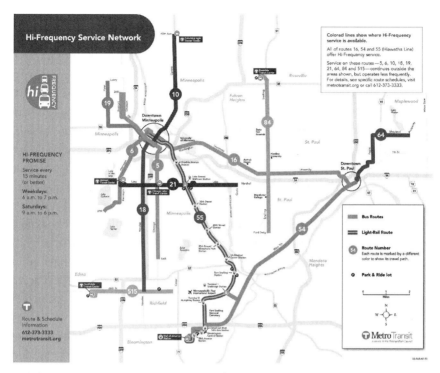

**Figure 7-2**  Frequent Network map for Minneapolis and St. Paul. *Source:* Metro Transit

busy to be waiting a long time or worrying about whether service quits running at 7:00 p.m. Where can I go on transit? Show me the network that's useful to me.

There are many people like that in our cities. With Frequent Network branding, transit agencies reach out to them, welcome them as customers, and show them that their transit system is simpler than it looks.

Frequent Network brands, once created, should be conveyed throughout the information system. On bus stop signs, for example, huge piles of route numbers effectively advertise the complexity of the network rather than its simplicity. Highlighting frequent services (and de-emphasizing peak-only ones) can help everyone see the services that are most likely to be useful to them. Transit agencies in Portland, Minneapolis–St. Paul, Salt Lake City, Montreal, and Adelaide, among others, use these techniques.

So, why isn't everyone doing Frequent Network branding by now? I've encountered two reasons—apart from sheer inertia—that agencies resist the practice. First, a Frequent Network map shows that frequency is very unevenly distributed over a transit system's area. Frequent service tends to be concentrated in areas of higher density, often in the older, core parts of big urban areas. You may not notice this on a map showing all the lines of a network, because there are usually transit lines of some kind everywhere. But on a Frequent Network map, like the one for Minneapolis–St. Paul in figure 7-2, it really jumps out at you. Someone in the north-central suburb of Roseville will look at the map in figure 7-2 and say: "Hey, why do we have only the tip of one Frequent line, when inner-city Minneapolis has lots of them?" Some transit agencies don't want to deal with this question, so it's tempting to avoid calling attention to where the frequent services are.

A better solution to that problem is to answer the objection. The objector is making a classic map-reading error, looking at map *area* as though it represented *population*. Suburbs like Roseville are less dense than inner Minneapolis, so that part of the map's area represents fewer people. There's nothing obviously unfair about having less service where there are fewer people. We'll dig deeper into perceptions of fairness in chapter 10.

Second, agencies who want to do Frequent Network branding get stuck trying to decide exactly what degree of frequency and span should count. They worry about whether the Frequent Network routes need to be frequent on weekends, and whether they need to be frequent until 7:00 p.m. or 9:00 p.m. or midnight. They wonder if 15-minute frequency should be adequate, whether it should really be twelve, or whether, facing budget cuts, they could get away with twenty. An overly forgiving definition will mean that the Frequent Network brand means so little that it doesn't reward the intended time-sensitive customer. An overly strict definition, on the other hand, might mean that only two or three lines in the existing network count.

My response to this problem is simple: start where you are. Pick a definition of Frequent Network that's reasonable for your current system and resources, to get the brand established. Advertise the brand honestly. Meanwhile, set long-term goals for increasing the standard of service that the brand represents. For example, in Canberra, Australia, the long-term Strategic Public Transport Network Plan (for which I was the lead planner) says that Frequent Network service should be every 15 minutes or better, 15 hours per day, seven days per week. Meanwhile, current practice is to settle for 15-minute frequency or better, 12 hours per day, weekdays only.

## The "New Route" Problem

When a group of citizens identifies the need for better transit from point A to point B, their proposal often takes the form of a new route or line from A to B. But if this proposed service overlaps other existing services, it's crucial to ask whether the overlap is a good idea. We are always trying to maximize frequency, but we can do that only by minimizing the number of miles (or kilometers) of distinct lines. Several possible solutions to this problem exist, but ignoring the problem isn't one of them. For more on this, see http://www.human transit.org/07box.html.

As long as we're honest about the boundaries of our existing brand while also asserting our long-term intentions for it, there isn't a problem.

Frequent Network branding can also help an agency align its short-term planning to its long-term planning. Long-term network plans need to identify where frequent service will be decades in the future, because this is an important input to land use planning, a process to which we'll return in chapters 14 and 16. Long-term plans only appear credible, though, if short-term planning is clearly following them.

Meanwhile, in the short-term, defining the Frequent Network is a crucial step toward recognizing the nature of the customer experience. Frequency often matters more than speed in determining your actual transit mobility—that is, how soon you'll get where you're going. Frequent Network branding is a key step in being honest about that. It shows that you, as an agency, value customers who value their own time, and who'll only use services that are there whenever they need them. It means your service is ready to be an instrument of freedom.

## WHAT RIVERS TEACH: BRANCHING AND DISSIPATION

In 2011, cartographer Daniel Huffman thought it would be interesting to draw river systems as though they were subways. Figure 7-3 shows part of his sketch of the Lower Mississippi.[4]

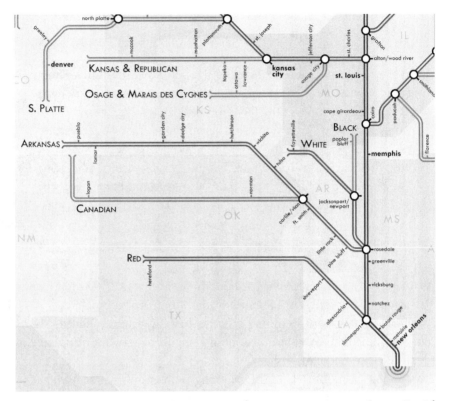

**Figure 7-3** Lower Mississippi River system, drawn as a transit map. *Source:* Daniel Huffman

It's a fun idea, but it also points to an important insight. If you travel upriver by boat, you expect the river to get smaller and smaller. Every time you reach a branching point, the volume of water in the two rivers in front of you is the same as the volume in the river behind you. If you keep going, you'll eventually reach a river that's too small for your boat. Transit is like that too, because *branching always divides frequency.*

This is one of those too-obvious points that is easy to miss in the heat of a transit debate. For example, in 2003, the BART system opened a new extension to San Francisco International Airport (SFO) and also to Millbrae, an important connection point with the Caltrain commuter rail system. The basic extension, southward from San Francisco, looks like the top image in figure 7-4. It's a triangle, with tracks from San Francisco to both SFO and Millbrae, and also direct tracks between Millbrae and SFO.

The *infrastructure* looks like this:

But the *service* will be one of these ...

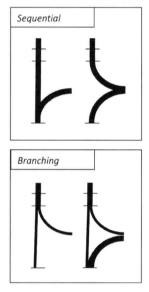

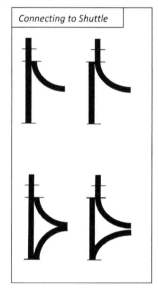

**Figure 7-4**
BART San Francisco Airport (SFO) terminus.

If you're unconsciously thinking like a motorist and looking at the top diagram as though it were a highway map, it looks fine. All the points on the map are directly connected to all the others. But transit can't run all of these connections at the same high frequency, because of the effect of branching. The actual pattern of service will have to be one of the images beneath it. In these images, *line width represents frequency*. (This is usually the best way to render frequency without color.)

For example, suppose you want service every 10 minutes to both SFO and Millbrae but you can afford only 10-minute frequency on the line through San Bruno and on to San Francisco. You have to run one of the two "sequential" options shown in figure 7-4: either run all service to Millbrae via SFO or run all service via SFO to Millbrae. Either SFO passengers or Millbrae passengers are going to hate you.

Alternatively, we could branch the service at San Bruno, sending half of it to SFO and half of it to Millbrae. But the branching will cut our frequency. If we can afford only 10-minute frequency through San Bruno, then we'll end up with 20-minute frequency at SFO and at Millbrae, which is at the very outer edge of anything that you would call "rapid transit."

Finally, we can run everything every 10 minutes by requiring some riders to make a connection. One side of the loop would have a shuttle train, while the other would have through service.

There is one other option, though it's not available for BART. You could split the train in half and send the front half on one branch and the rear half on the other. This is very tricky; it requires a driver in position ready to take half of the train when it arrives. It's also hard to separate a train without at least a minute of delay, at least for the rear half of the divided train.

To sum up, we should be suspicious whenever we see a branch drawn as though one line can effortlessly divide into two equal lines, because this *always* means one of three things:

- Points beyond the branching point have less frequent service.
- One of the branches operates as a shuttle, requiring a connection.
- In a few rare cases, the train itself comes apart, with some cars proceeding along one branch and some along the other.

Geometrically, it *has* to mean one of these three things, and it may not be the one you prefer. So, before you decide whether the service is useful to you, or whether you support a proposed transit project whose map looks like this, you may want to ask which of these it is.

# 8

# THE OBSTACLE COURSE: SPEED, DELAY, AND RELIABILITY

When we think about transportation, no concept seems more fundamental than speed. We just want to get there, and speed sounds like the most direct measure of how soon we will. Indeed, if you divide the distance you travel by how long it took, you have something that you can fairly call the *average speed* of your trip.

But speed is also a symbol of liberty, autonomy, and power. When Tracy Chapman sings that "we'll get a fast car,"[1] she means that we'll break out of poverty and create a new life. So we should be a little suspicious of speed. Speed sounds like a simple thing to measure, but because it carries this symbolic weight, it's easy to mistake speed for a transit service's actual ability to get us somewhere. As we've already seen, people thinking like motorists often focus too much on transit's speed and not enough on frequency. Another common mistake is to care too much about top speed, as a capability of the transit technology, which may not be relevant to how that vehicle is likely to function in service.

Speed can also be a source of fear. When planners talk about trying to speed up transit, someone always imagines that we're talking about raising the top speed, that transit is going to be "speeding" in the sense of driving too fast. Normal operations never require "speeding" in this sense. It's the stops, and other sources of delay, that really determine how soon you'll get there.

## THE REAL PROBLEM: DELAY

In most urban transit, what matters is not speed but *delay*. Most transit technologies can go as fast as it's safe to go in an urban setting—either on roads or on rails. What matters is mostly what can get in their way, how often they will stop, and for how long. So when we work to speed up transit, we focus on removing delays.

Delay is also the main source of problems of reliability. Reliability and average speed are different concepts, but both are undermined by the same kinds of delay, and when we reduce delay, service usually runs both faster and more reliably.[a]

Longer-distance travel between cities is different, so analogies from those services can mislead. Airplanes, oceangoing ships, and intercity trains all spend long stretches of time at their maximum possible speed, with nothing to stop for and nothing to get in their way. Urban transit is different because (a) it stops much more frequently, so top speed matters less than the stops, and (b) it tends to be in situations that restrict its speed, including various kinds of congestion. Even in a rail transit system with an unobstructed path, the volume of trains going through imposes some limits, because you have to maintain a safe spacing between them even as they stop and start at stations.

This chapter is about *routine delay*—delay that is a typical part of the operations of a transit line. There are also several kinds of *exceptional delay*, including accidents, medical emergencies, extreme weather, breakdowns, construction, police activity, and strikes or work slowdowns by unionized labor.

Delay can also be the result of large-scale operational failures, such as the failure to put a scheduled vehicle into service at all. Those all need monitoring at the citywide or agencywide level, but they aren't a feature of a particular line or running way, so we can't usefully deal with them here.

---

[a] There's one exception to the principle that speed improvements are usually reliability improvements. One way to improve reliability is to write a slower schedule, so that services that were running late can now be declared on time. This can sometimes be the only option, but it also amounts to a lowering of expectations. Transit agencies that value quality should never do this without raising an alarm and having some public discussion, which could lead to support for more active interventions to improve both reliability and speed.

## THREE SOURCES OF ROUTINE DELAY AND THREE KINDS OF RUNNING WAY

There are three big categories of routine delay:

- *Traffic delay* is caused by the interference of other vehicles.
- *Signal delay* is caused by required stops at signals.
- *Passenger-stop delay* is caused by stops for passenger boarding and alighting.

These three kinds of delay define the three fundamentally different kinds of running way (figure 8-1). A *running way* is a traffic lane for a bus, a track for a railcar, or the water for ferries. Vukan Vuchic[2] calls them classes A, B, and C, and since no concise names for them exist, I'll use his terms. A transit service—bus or rail—may be

- *class A: exclusive and separated.* "Exclusive" means that no other traffic operates in its lane or on its track. "Separated" means that no cross

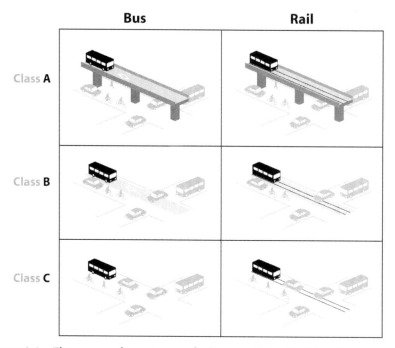

**Figure 8-1**  Three types of running way for bus or rail. *Credit:* Alfred Twu

traffic intersects it. Class A services experience passenger-stop delay, but no other delay types, except to the degree that transit vehicles may sometimes obstruct one another. Rail rapid transit that uses a "third rail" power source—such as most big-city subways—is almost always class A, but there are also some class A busways and light rail segments.

- *class B: exclusive but not separated.* Here, transit has its lane or track to itself but must interact with cross traffic, usually at signals. Class B running way protects transit from traffic delay but exposes it to signal delay and passenger-stop delay. Most North American light rail is in this category, as are many surface busways, such as the Los Angeles Orange Line.
- *class C: mixed traffic, neither exclusive nor separated.* Conventional bus and streetcar operations that share their lane with traffic are in this category.

Note that there are bus and rail services in all three categories. If you perceive a rail rapid transit system to be very fast and reliable, that's probably because it runs in a class A running way (often underground or elevated) where passenger stops are the main source of delay, and also because it has optimized passenger stopping time using tools we'll explore below. If you perceive your city buses to be unreliable, that's probably because they run in a class C environment, exposed to all three kinds of delay: traffic, signals, and passenger stops.

But you can put rail in a class C situation—that's what most North American streetcars are—and you'll get class C delays as a result. You can also put buses in a class A situation, in busways that don't intersect streets. Long segments of these can be found in Brisbane, Ottawa, Bogotá, Los Angeles, and Pittsburgh. The bus lines that use these segments often run in class C segments as well, so their reliability may be compromised by what happens in those segments. But while running in these separated busways, they experience only passenger-stop delay, so they are capable of the same reliability, and often the same running time, as rapid transit services.

## THE SEVEN DEADLY DELAYS

Class A or B running way offers complete protection from one or more types of delay. But even if we don't have the ideal running way, we can use several tools to reduce delay. To use them, we have to break down the three main types of delay into seven types, each addressed with different tools:

- *Traffic delay* is of two kinds:
  - *Congestion.* The entire street or lane is slowed by vehicles moving below their ideal speed. Protecting transit from congestion is the main function of class A and B facilities. Class A usually means elevated or underground, which is very expensive, so much effort goes into class B facilities, usually on-street transit lanes, which can be either bus lanes or rail lines not mixed with traffic.
  - *Friction.* Friction is delay caused by individual vehicles, such as delivery trucks and taxis stopping for customers, cars engaged in parallel parking movements, car doors being opened into your lane, slow cyclists sharing the traffic lane, and so on. On busy streets, an advantage of putting transit lanes in the center, rather than on the side, is that it eliminates most friction. A transit lane along the curb might be called "B-minus," because while the lane is mostly clear for transit, cars do merge across it and may block it during pickup/dropoff activities and turns.
- *Signal delay.* Buses, streetcars, and light rail may sometimes have to stop at traffic signals. Only class A systems eliminate signal delay. In class B and C running ways, however, signal delay can be reduced through a range of *signal priority* tools, which give transit a faster trip through signals. For example, green times may be extended so that a transit vehicle can get through, or transit may be given a short lane for bypassing traffic stopped at a signal, combined with a special signal that lets transit proceed before the general traffic. Signal priority can be justified by a goal of managing a street for person trips rather than vehicle trips. Dumb signals treat all vehicles equally, whereas signal priority gives preference to transit because it represents more people. The Los Angeles Metro Rapid, for example, is mostly in mixed traffic but does get an advantage at signals. You might call this arrangement "C-plus."
- *Passenger-stop delay* includes all delay related to stops for passenger boarding and alighting. Most stop-related delay is *dwell*, which means time spent stopped at a station.

- *Dwell due to boarding/alighting* is determined by the limitations of space on the vehicle, and on the sidewalk or platform, as well as the number and width of the doors.
- *Dwell due to fare collection* is a massive source of delay on conventional "pay the driver" systems, especially where this requires all customers to board through the front door. Smartcards (chapter 11) will reduce this delay by making the transactions much faster and permitting customers to do the transaction at any door. "Proof of payment" systems, in which riders do not have to show the driver a ticket but are subject to random inspection, can also eliminate much fare collection delay.
- *Acceleration/deceleration.* Some delay related to passenger stops happens in the transitions between cruising speed and a full stop. In rapid transit systems that are protected from traffic and signal delay, this can be a significant factor. Electric propulsion technologies—bus or rail—are especially good at accelerating from stops, even uphill and with heavy loads. This category is a nuisance because it's a kind of passenger-stop delay but is hard to separate from traffic delay in class C (transit in mixed traffic) settings.

Those three factors add up to the total delay due to one passenger stop, but the total stop-related delay along a line, of course, is the delay per stop times the number of stops. So we must also care about:

- *Stop spacing.* As we saw in chapter 5, putting stops closer together slows service down, so optimal stop spacing is as wide as possible while still making it possible for the intended customers to get to the service. Remember: the other kinds of passenger-stop delays are *added* to one another, but they are all potentially *multiplied* by this one. That's why the unglamorous work of stop spacing is so important to get right (and why I devoted chapter 5 to it).

In rapid transit operations, passenger stop delay becomes even more onerous. Many subway lines experience severe overcrowding during peak periods, and transit agencies try to put as many trains through the subway as possible. Automatic Train Control systems make it possible to run trains much closer together than you could with manual control; in some, you can put a train through every ninety seconds. With all other delay types removed, these systems become intensely sensitive to dwell time at stations. Any incident, even just an unusually slow boarding/alighting process, generates an immediate traffic jam of trains in the tunnel behind. Conversely, any strategy that will speed up boarding and alighting allows trains to be run closer together, increasing the potential capacity of the subway.

Rapid transit, of course, is a class A service that suffers only from passenger-stop delays. What can we do to improve delay on current class C services, where all seven types of delay are at work?

For a vivid example, consider San Francisco's busy Van Ness Avenue, a six- to eight-lane street lined with tall buildings, where crowded buses struggle at midday average speeds of just over 6 miles per hour (mph) (10 km/h), compared to 10 mph (16 km/h) for cars.[3] There is no parallel rapid transit option for travel in this busy corridor.

When making the case for a transit lane, the transit agency studied how the buses on this crucial street were spending their time. Running northbound during the midday, on a segment that is 2.0 miles (3.2 km) long, they found that the 19-minute bus ride consisted of the following:

- 9.3 minutes spent moving (including time below the speed limit due to traffic delay or acceleration/deceleration for passenger stops)
- 4.6 minutes waiting for signals (signal delay)
- 0.3 minute stopped due to traffic (more traffic delay)
- 4.9 minutes at dwell (passenger-stop delay)

So, in round numbers, the Van Ness buses spend only about half their time in motion. They spend a quarter of their time dwelling at passenger stops, and a quarter of their time waiting for signals. It's a grim picture for one of San Francisco's most important transit links.

We can understand traffic delay a little more precisely by looking at how fast the service would have been if there were no passenger stops or signals. In that case, the bus would have taken 9.3 minutes to go 2.0 miles (3.2 km), which is 12.9 mph (20.8 km/h). The speed limit of this street is 35 mph (56 km/h), so at the speed limit, the same trip would have taken 3.4 minutes. So, of the 9.3 minutes that the bus spends in motion, 5.9 minutes are lost (relative to the speed limit) in traffic delay, in addition to the 0.3 minute that the bus was completely stopped due to traffic.

So, here's the whole picture of how travel time breaks down on this important link. Of our total travel time, 18 percent would have been needed if we had gone the speed limit. The rest is delay, which consists of:

- Passenger stop delay (26%)
- Signal delay (24%)
- Traffic delay, including acceleration/deceleration (32%)

The message here is that much can be accomplished by attacking any of the main delay classes: traffic, passenger stops, and signals.

In the specific case of Van Ness, attacking signal delay is tricky. The street is part of a grid with many interlocking patterns of signal progression, and these would be disrupted if transit tried to take too much priority at signals. What's more, many of the intersecting streets also have important transit lines on them, so an overly strong system of signal priority would shift problems from Van Ness to the intersecting lines.

So, San Francisco transit planners focused mainly on traffic delay and passenger-stop delay. That's why they arrived at a recommendation of Bus Rapid Transit, specifically a median bus lane (protected from the friction that afflicts side bus lanes) with a proof-of-payment fare system that would eliminate the delays associated with front-door, "pay the driver" fare collection. The system would also reduce passenger stop delays by widening the stop spacing, creating a service that's worth walking to.

Van Ness is a particularly challenging corridor, with a combination of heavy ridership, closely spaced signals, and heavy traffic. But many class C operations in urban settings have similar outcomes. For example, in the dense urban parts of its original alignment, the Portland Streetcar is as slow as the Van Ness buses, even though it is spared most fare collection delay since it uses a proof-of-payment system.[4]

## THE CASE FOR TRANSIT LANES

Like most city streets with intense transit needs, Van Ness Avenue will never be wider. A total width of 125 feet (38 m) will need to be apportioned among all the uses of the street, including not just travel lanes but also pedestrian space, on-street parking, and other features that create a great street, such as landscaping.

**Table 8-1**   Person Trips on Van Ness Avenue, San Francisco, 2005

| | Northbound Lanes (all five streets combined) | Persons per Hour in Cars | Persons per Hour on Transit | % on Transit |
|---|---|---|---|---|
| P.M. Peak Hour | 7 | 178,700 | 26,900 | 13% |
| All Day | 7 | 36,500 | 6,500 | 15% |

On any great urban street, every part of the current use has its fierce defenders. Local merchants will do anything to keep the on-street parking in front of their businesses. Motorists will worry (not always correctly) that losing a lane of traffic means more congestion. Removing landscaping can be controversial, especially if mature trees are involved.

To win space for transit lanes in this environment, we usually have to talk about fairness. Table 8-1 shows 2005 figures representing how transit and motorists share the space on Van Ness and five adjacent parallel streets during the afternoon rush hour.[b]

What if we turned a northbound traffic lane on Van Ness into a transit lane? We'd be taking 14 percent (one-seventh) of the lane capacity of these streets to serve about 14 percent of the people who *already* travel in those lanes, namely, the people already using transit. Sounds fair, doesn't it?

Even in 2005, on buses that get through Van Ness only about twice as fast as most people can walk, the transit riders were one-seventh of everyone moving in vehicles, so it seems only fair to give them one-seventh of the travel lanes by setting aside one northbound lane for transit.[c]

Obviously, though, the real payoff would come from the dramatic improvement in speed and reliability, which would attract more passengers to the service. Before long, the transit lanes would be moving *more* people than the car lanes. Once you decide that your streets are designed for people movement rather than vehicle movement, turning car lanes into transit lanes not only is fair but is also the most effective way to maximize the total

---

[b] The five parallel streets are also designed for heavy traffic movement, so traffic can move readily from one to another to find the fastest way. For this reason, the band of streets needs to be thought of together when apportioning street space.

[c] To be precise, this would involve shifting the local buses on the adjacent and parallel Polk Street to a Van Ness transit lane, because they (and Polk Street car traffic) are part of the volumes counted here.

number of people who can move along the street. And if you want to grow your economy without growing congestion, that's the output you need to focus on.

The basic math of urban transit lanes can sometimes be that simple, and that compelling. In dense cities with heavy transit demand, the case for a transit lane may be based on just a few numbers:

- What percentage of the people who are already traveling down the street's traffic lanes are on transit instead of in cars? Don't these people deserve at least the same percentage of road width set aside for them, especially since they can use this space more efficiently?
- How much faster will transit be if it has an exclusive lane? How will this change people's actual mobility—say, the extent of the area that *you* can get to in 30 minutes on transit?

When you hear of a transit lane proposal, ask yourself: If transit were that fast and reliable, wouldn't more people use it? Might *you* even use it, instead of driving, taking a taxi, or whatever it is that you do?

Of course, your favorite boulevard may yield much different numbers. You may not have enough existing riders on transit to justify the lane, so you will have to depend on ridership projection and quantified mobility improvement to show that if the lane were created, it would in fact attract its fair share of travelers to justify its share of the width of the street.

From a sustainability perspective, of course, you can argue that you don't even need to be carrying that share of passengers, or at least not at first. To the extent that collective purposes are served by encouraging people to use transit, you can apportion street space to transit in order to achieve that outcome in the long run, regardless of what the ridership is now. It's the same principle that leads to preferred parking for carpools and electric cars.

## THE "EMPTY" TRANSIT LANE PROBLEM

Much of the resistance to transit lanes comes from how they appear to motorists. If you are sitting in stopped traffic and a transit lane is right next to you, the transit lane will look empty most of the time. Now and then a bus will flash past, but if you're sitting still and the bus is going at full speed, you'll mostly be gazing at empty pavement.

Motorists who see that often decide that the bus lane isn't working. Surely, if it were working right, you'd see buses in it most of the time, wouldn't you? Wrong. Fast-moving buses are a quick blur to the stopped motorist. *Only a blocked or failing bus lane appears to be full of buses.*

For example, in the photo of Hoddle Street in Melbourne shown in figure 8-2, the bus lane is carrying far more passengers than a traffic lane.[5] In fact, in this peak period condition, it's carrying more than all three traffic lanes combined. Now imagine this photo with only one bus instead of the three that are easily visible. The bus lane would still be carrying as many people as one car lane, but it would *look* empty, especially from the vantage point of someone in a stopped car. The problem is even worse on freeways, where buses at cruising speed pass stopped traffic so fast that they barely register to the stopped motorist.

**Figure 8-2** Hoddle Street near Collingwood Town Hall in Melbourne, during a weekday afternoon commute. *Source:* Graham Currie

In most cities, the motorist's perception is so dominant that their confusions can become political imperatives. Wherever transit lanes operate, elected officials get angry letters about how empty they are, as though this implies that they are wasting space. Planning studies for transit lanes sometimes refer to "empty lane syndrome," as though this common fallacy in the motorist's perception is an objective technical problem. It is certainly a political problem, but it's one rooted in ignorance, and only information will combat it.

# 9

# DENSITY DISTRACTIONS

In chapter 5, we looked at the fixed radius around transit stops, the area where people are likely to find the stop useful. Transit's market depends on how many people are going to or from places in that area. How many people live there? How many people work there? How many students are in schools there? How much shopping goes on? Planners ask these questions to gauge the size of the transit market and (more perilously) to predict ridership.

We can quarrel about how far we should expect people to walk, bike, or drive to a stop, but whatever distance that is, it defines a finite area. And when we ask how many people, jobs, and so forth are in a finite area, we're asking about *density*. Because there are several ways to measure density, which will yield very different impressions, we need to be precise about how density matters for transit.

In this chapter and the next, I will talk mostly about residential density. This is not the only kind of density that matters to transit; the density of jobs and other activities is equally fundamental.[1] Density is also not the sole determinant of ridership; service matters, obviously, but so do urban design features such as walkability, as well as the pricing of transit compared to a customer's alternatives.

But when we want to talk about the essence of density, we usually talk about residential density, partly because it's easiest to measure and partly because it arouses intense popular interest. Our political system represents people where they live, not where they work, so while commercial density is hugely important to ridership as well, it's the residential development pattern that drives our representative politics.

As I'll argue in chapter 10, a strong relationship between residential density and transit outcomes is both empirically and geometrically obvious. This is not to say that other factors don't matter. It does mean that we have to be able to talk about density, and residential density is the easiest way to illustrate the fundamental point about how density of all kinds operates.

## DENSITY AND EMOTION

Density—especially residential density—arouses strong emotions.

Most obviously, whenever we talk about urban form, people hear us making judgments about their homes. I can stand in front of a group of citizens and talk about how a certain kind of development pattern implies certain consequences for transit, and thus for sustainability, and thus for the human future. As we talk, it may appear that we're having a thoughtful and educational discussion about good and bad design. But some people in the audience have chosen to make their homes in the very development pattern that I'm describing, and to those people, I'm saying that their home is good or bad.

Once you hear that, you're likely to have a strong emotional reaction that makes you deaf to rational argument. On some level, consciously or unconsciously, you're going to feel as though I'd walked into your living room and told you that your decor is not just ugly but a threat to civilization. We all feel protective of our homes.

Density also evokes fear. One common distortion of the sustainable transport agenda is to claim that the goal is coercive, that planners are going to "force" people to give up their homes and live in towers. For the record, I—like most urbanists—have no interest in forcing anyone to do anything. Rather, I want people to make free but informed choices, based on a full understanding of the consequences. People must be free to live at low densities, but that choice has profound impacts—on transit and other public services—that need to be understood.

## DENSITY'S MEASUREMENT PROBLEM

In his 2010 book *Transport for Suburbia*, Paul Mees notices a fallacy that seems to be shared by transit advocates and car advocates. Both sides of this great debate agree that *effective transit requires high density*.

Sustainability advocates want higher urban densities for a range of reasons, and viability of public transit is certainly one of them. Meanwhile, advocates of car dominance want to argue that existing low densities are a fact of life; since transit needs high density, they say, it's best to go on planning for the dominance of cars.

Mees calls on his fellow transit advocates to let go of the idea that good transit requires high densities:

> The central argument of this book is that density is not destiny. Transport policy itself has a bigger impact on transport patterns than urban planners have realized, and suburbs don't have to be totally reliant on the car. Planners who insist that car dominance can only be addressed by impossibly large increases in density may actually be entrenching the problem they are trying to solve.[2]

Mees is right that "density is not destiny." Cities of any density can make better or worse transit choices and achieve different outcomes as a result. But density is still an overwhelming force in determining the possibilities and outcomes of transit, and we can't begin to make good transit decisions until we understand it.

At the core of Mees's book is a table that compares the gross residential density of several urban areas with the transit performance in each area.[3] The point of the table is to suggest that there's really no relationship between the two. Table 9-1 shows a few of Mees's numbers.[a]

The density figures seem calculated to shock. *Los Angeles is denser than New York?* Yes, that's what happens when you average over a vast urban

---

[a] In table 9-1, "Metro Area" is my term for what Mees's table calls "City." It refers to the entire urbanized area around a city, regardless of government boundaries. Think of it as the continuous patch of lights that you can see from an airplane at night. "Transit mode share for work trips" is the percentage of trips to work that go by transit, as opposed to car, walking, biking, and so forth. Trips to work are not the only ones that matter, but they are the only ones that are measured consistently.

**Table 9-1**   Metro Area Density and Transit Performance

| Metro Area | Population Density (pop/ha) | Transit Mode Share for Work Trips |
|---|---|---|
| Los Angeles | 27.3 | 4.7 |
| New York | 20.5 | 24.8 |
| Las Vegas | 17.7 | 4.1 |
| Vancouver | 17.0 | 16.5 |

Source: Paul Mees, *Transport for Suburbia: Beyond the Automobile Age* (London: Earthscan, 2010).

area. "New York" in this table is not just New York City but the entire metro area stretching across three states, much of it very low density. Most of that area is irrelevant to New York's transit outcomes, because it doesn't have much service and doesn't represent very many people. So it's misleading to cite these average density numbers as evidence about density's relevance to transit one way or the other.

It's inevitable that in comparisons between cities, we're going to hear average density figures—for example, the whole population of a metro area divided by its land area. These figures are better than nothing when it comes to making global comparisons. For example, the databases created by Peter Newman and Jeffrey Kenworthy, which compare sustainability indicators for entire urban areas worldwide, are useful in showing how a range of outcomes, including transit performance, can vary with density.[4]

But averages are often dangerous, especially for transit. Averaging sounds like a credible way to draw a simple fact out of a huge and diverse reality, but in this case, averages are just not the fact that matters.

What matters to transit is the *density around the transit system's stops and stations*, especially those that offer a high level of mobility. To talk about this coherently, we need to be able to measure density in a very fine-grained way. If you believe that one quarter mile (400 m) is a reasonable walking distance (and if not, substitute whatever number you prefer), then the question that matters is: "How many residents and jobs are within one quarter mile (400 m) of a stop?"

This fixed radius has a fixed area, so the answer to this question can fairly be called a density. But it's a very specialized kind of density, one that must be measured right at the boundary of the desired radius. Even more precisely, it should be measured along walkable paths, as we did in chapter 5. Not many governments have the tools to do this, but these tools are improving.[b]

## DENSITY BY AREA OR BY POPULATION?

If the density measurement that matters to transit is so specialized and local, does that mean that all citywide generalizations and comparisons are meaningless? Rhetorically, we do need to talk about the difference in density from one city to another. In some situations, if you don't have a simple number to make your citywide point, you won't get a word in.

When we need a quick number for a sound bite, we should resist talking about average density and talk instead about percentages of the population who are in different density situations. The average density of our city may tell us nothing about the prospects for transit, but if we speak instead of the *percentage of citizens who live at high density*, we get closer.

Thinking this way would give us a more accurate comparison of New York and Los Angeles, even while thinking of both as giant metro areas. Figure 9-1 is a simple graph that shows how the population in each city is distributed by density.

Greater Los Angeles has a huge population living at medium densities, with almost nobody at the highest densities. New York shows a much broader distribution, including substantial numbers living at the extreme densities characterized by the massed towers of Manhattan. Here is a much better basis for sound bites explaining why New York has a much higher

---

[b] Governments keep track of their current and projected development using models that divide up the city into zones and record the population, jobs, and so on of each. Governments that are thinking in car-dominated terms may have quite large zones, because fine detail doesn't matter much for road planning. For example, if you plan a huge industrial park next to a particular freeway off-ramp, the model may show the entire park as one zone, because all that really matters is the traffic that the whole park will generate at the freeway interchange. Transit, by contrast, reacts to very small differences in walking distance, so it needs a much more fine-grained breakdown, approaching the level of the development parcel. A good signal that a government is serious about transit (and walking) is the small size of its transportation analysis zones.

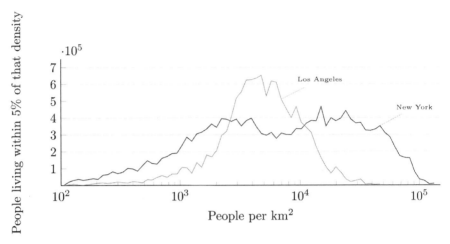

**Figure 9-1** Distribution of metro area populations by residential density. *Credit:* Fedor Manin. *Source:* 2000 US Census

transit performance than Los Angeles. What matters is not the *average* density but the percentage of the population living at higher densities.

Of course, this doesn't mean that the Los Angeles transit task is hopeless—only that the city shouldn't be comparing itself to New York. The medium densities at which most Los Angeles residents live—reflecting a range from bungalows on very small lots to midrise apartment buildings—are plenty dense for intense transit ridership on buses and the occasional rapid transit line. But Los Angeles doesn't need anything like Manhattan's thick braid of parallel subways. Manhattan is the outlier, of course. By North American or even European standards, Los Angeles has superb transit potential.

## IS LOW DENSITY A PROBLEM FOR TRANSIT? IT DEPENDS

In any case, don't be distracted by the average density of your entire urban area, or even of your city. Forget, too, about the notion that transit advocates want to force "everyone" to live at higher density. It's the density near stops and stations that will determine the size of a city's transit market, and thus its transit outcomes. *Your city can still include as much low-density area as you like.* If that area doesn't demand much transit service, and doesn't extend into transit station areas, it will have little impact on transit ridership one way or the other.

Of course, low-density areas do sometimes touch station areas and do usually demand some transit service, and in those cases, they can negatively affect transit performance. The question of how much service to run in low-density areas is part of one of the most challenging plumber's questions: are we planning for ridership or for coverage? It's time to confront that question.

# 10

# RIDERSHIP OR COVERAGE? THE CHALLENGE OF SERVICE ALLOCATION

If your city or region is big enough to have transit at all, it's big enough to have debates about how to apportion service among different communities. Every transit system serves areas where ridership is high and other areas where it's lower. Should higher ridership lead to better service? If not, how should a transit system divide up its resources among the communities it serves? To answer this unavoidable question, you have to think about why you're running public transit at all.[a]

Most government functions have clear purposes. Everyone understands the purpose of the sewer system, the fire department, and the tax collector. These agencies may also be asked to satisfy other values, such as fair employment laws and good environmental practices, but these other values are clearly distinct from the primary mission of each agency. The external values are important, but they affect *how* the job is to be done. They rarely raise confusion about *what* the job is.

---

[a] This chapter is based on my 2008 paper "Purpose Driven Public Transport: Creating a Clear Conversation about Public Transport Goals," *Journal of Transport Geography* 16 (2008): 436–42. That paper contains additional detail on techniques for developing the suggested policies.

Sometimes, though, an agency is given two jobs that simply can't be done at the same time. The U.S. Forest Service, for example, is expected to both protect forests and sell timber. The U.S. Federal Aviation Administration's conflicting missions—to promote the airline industry while also regulating it—is another example that is sometimes in the news.

When an agency faces contradictory missions, the first impulse is to find ways of making the missions *seem* harmonious. Some U.S. Forest Service signs proclaim that the National Forest is a "Land of Many Uses," which may give the brief impression that logging, mining, recreation, and conservation all go on in perfect harmony. Eventually, though, the reality of the contradiction overwhelms the best rhetorical efforts.

Transit also faces a contradictory mission. You can see it in two types of goals that most agencies adopt but rarely reconcile. Most agencies have two goals that sound something like this:

1.  Serve all parts of our community.
2.  Maximize ridership with our fixed service budget.

The first goal, called a *Coverage Goal*, says that the agency must serve everyone in its service area—that is, everyone who pays taxes to the agency and votes for the elected officials who will make decisions about transit. Implicit in the Coverage Goal is that some service must be provided *regardless of how few people use it.*

Coverage Goals arise from two political sources. First, they reflect concerns about *equity* ("we pay taxes too, so we deserve service even if we don't use it much"). Second, they arise from a *social-service objective* that focuses on meeting the needs of people who are especially reliant on transit, whether due to age, disability, poverty, or some other condition. Arguments for coverage-based service refer not just to how many people need it but also to the severity of that need. Whenever people defend a low-ridership service in terms of how badly they need it, and how hard their lives would be without it, you are in the presence of a Coverage Goal.

The second goal is a *Ridership Goal*. It calls for deploying service the way private business would, with the aim of the highest possible ridership for a given service budget. The Ridership Goal is implicit in measures such as "farebox recovery," the percentage of operating cost recovered by fares.

In areas where demand is high, the Ridership Goal provides very intense service. But in places where demand will always be low, an agency pursuing the Ridership Goal would offer no service at all, just as a competitive airline will not fly into towns that are too small to fill its planes.

Ridership is not exactly the right word, but the right word, *productivity*, will sound too bureaucratic to many readers. Coverage service aims for riders, too, but implicitly judges its success not on how many people it carries but on how badly they need the service, and on how much of the city or region has been covered. The Ridership Goal, by contrast, is to carry *as many riders as possible for the fixed budget*. Since operating budgets are driven mostly by labor cost, which varies by the hour, the Ridership Goal is mostly focused on maximizing ridership per service hour, where a "service hour" is one transit vehicle operating for one hour. So when I use "Ridership" (capitalized) as the opposite of "Coverage," this means ridership *for a fixed operating budget*.

Ridership Goals serve two major public interests. First, if your aim is to *compete successfully with cars* to achieve environmental benefits, a Ridership Goal is most likely to do that. But if you're thinking about transit like a business, you want *maximum fare revenue*, and in that case you'll also be drawn to the Ridership Goal.

When we state each goal separately, both are almost universally popular. Many people assume that their transit agencies are already pursuing both goals at once. For example, transit is often criticized for carrying too few riders with its resources.[1] This criticism assumes that the transit agency is *trying* to carry as many riders as possible as its single overriding goal, which is almost never true.

Often, a transit agency will adopt both goals in some form but will never resolve the conflict between them. With this move, they hurl their staff in opposite directions at once. In the worst cases, the contradictory goals can make it impossible for a competent staff to do their jobs, which in turn can cause the loss of the best employees. Nobody wants to work at a job where every time they do anything to pursue goal A, they will be blasted for undermining the conflicting goal B, and vice versa.

But why can't we have it both ways? Why can't we both serve everyone *and* maximize ridership? To see why, let's compare two idealized neighborhoods: Denseville and Sparseville (figure 10-1).

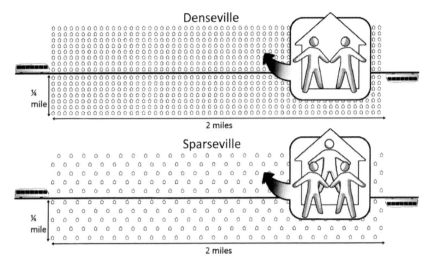

**Figure 10-1** Denseville and Sparseville. *Credit:* Erin Walsh

## DENSEVILLE AND SPARSEVILLE: UNAVOIDABLE CHOICES

Denseville and Sparseville are both 2 miles[b] long and one half mile wide, so they're 1 square mile in area. Their rectangular shape means that we can run a transit line lengthwise through the middle of each and the whole community will be within a quarter mile of it. At this scale, let's not worry about the stop spacing. As we saw in chapter 5, the edge of the served area is actually jagged, based on the exact locations of stops, but for this chapter's purposes we can ignore that detail.

Denseville and Sparseville are the same size and shape, but Denseville is twice as dense. In Sparseville, there are only 7,500 people per square mile, but in Denseville there are 15,000. Denseville is a mix of small bungalows, duplexes, and small apartment buildings, whereas Sparseville is almost entirely made up of single-family homes, some on large lots.

There's another difference that can cause confusion. Smaller housing units tend, in general, to house fewer people. Denseville is more likely to have people living alone, childless couples, and so forth, while Sparseville homes are more likely to house larger families or groups. We need to be

---

[b] To avoid clutter, I omit metric conversions of the simple distances used in this section. A mile is about 1.6 km. A square mile is about 2.6 square km or 259 hectares.

careful about this because residential density is sometimes described as population density (people per acre or hectare) and sometimes as housing density (dwelling units per acre or hectare). So let's assume, for the sake of simplicity, that on average there are two people per dwelling unit in Denseville, and three people per dwelling unit in Sparseville.

So, while Denseville has twice as many *people* as Sparseville, it has triple the number of housing units. The 15,000 people of Denseville live, two to a unit on average, in 7,500 housing units, whereas the 7,500 people of Sparseville live, three to a unit on average, in 2,500 housing units. (Don't try to count the little houses in my drawings; they're not trying to be accurate to that level of detail.)

Finally, let's assume that people in both Denseville and Sparseville are equally inclined to use transit. For example, let's say that on average, 5 percent of the people in each neighborhood will typically make one two-way transit trip each day. In Denseville (population 15,000), our 2-mile segment of transit line will attract 1,500 daily boardings, whereas in Sparseville (population 7,500), it will attract 750 boardings.[c] (Each round-trip, of course, is two boardings.)

So far, both line segments have the same speed and frequency, so they cost the same to operate. So, the *ridership per unit of operating cost* will be twice as high in Denseville as in Sparseville. That means the "farebox return," the percentage of operating cost paid by fares, will also be twice as high in Denseville, since we have the same operating cost but twice as many riders. To put it another way, the *operating cost per rider* will be twice as high in Sparseville as in Denseville.

By now, Sparseville and Denseville may be reminding you of certain neighborhoods in your own city. And if I'm explaining all this in a presentation to the elected officials who govern your transit system, the Sparseville representatives in the room are starting to look a little tense.

Every large transit agency has to talk about the fact that ridership is higher in some places than in others, and they often find it hard to do that without implying that either (a) there's something wrong with Sparseville or (b) there's something wrong with how they're serving Sparseville.

The real explanation is simpler than that: *Denseville has more riders because it has more people, and more activities, in the fixed area within walking*

---

[c] A boarding is the event of one person stepping onto a transit vehicle.

*distance of any transit stop.* If everyone in these debates could keep that basic geometric fact in mind, we'd have fewer hurt feelings all around.

## DENSEVILLE'S INTENSIFICATION EFFECTS

Up to now, we've assumed that everyone in both communities is equally likely to use public transit. But that assumption is not quite right, because the difference in density implies other important differences between these two communities.

Private cars, which require space for parking, are easy to maintain in Sparseville, because there's plenty of room for them. Owning a car in Denseville is more of a hassle. Denseville residents who drive are more likely to "pay" for parking—either in money, via paid parking lots or permits, or in time, by having to drive around for a long time before finding a spot.

Denseville residents also have less need to drive. A Denseville resident can probably walk or bike to a grocery store and some other necessities of life, while most Sparseville residents need cars to reach these things. Because there is more walking in Denseville, there are likely to be better sidewalks with more lighting. High density means more pedestrians, and that means walking feels safer, because you are less likely to be totally alone as a pedestrian on the street. These features are crucial parts of an attractive transit experience, because every transit rider is also a pedestrian.

Because of these differences, all of which tend to follow from the difference in density, Denseville residents typically have lower rates of car ownership. It is not that they can't afford cars. They simply don't need cars as much as Sparseville residents do. In Denseville, a family may need only one car for two or three adults, while in Sparseville there may be a car for every adult, or even more.

Up to now, we've assumed that Denseville and Sparseville residents are equally likely to use transit, but clearly that can't be right. An individual resident of Denseville is more likely to find transit attractive than an individual in Sparseville. So the *rate of transit use per citizen* will be higher in Denseville.

A 1996 study by Parsons Brinckerhoff found exactly that: transit ridership per person rises directly with density.[2] Note carefully what this is saying. We've seen that ridership rises with density because density means more people, but that's a different point. We're saying that *each* of those people is more likely to use transit if he or she lives in a denser area.

Now the ridership on our 2-mile segment of line can be calculated like this:

Ridership = Population × Rate of Transit Use per Person

These two communities are each 1 square mile in area, so in this case the population *is* the density, since we're measuring density in persons per square mile. But as we have seen, the *rate* of transit use per person also varies with density. So it should not surprise us that all other things being equal, ridership often seems to vary with the square of the density. Denseville is only twice as dense as Sparseville, but Denseville's transit ridership on the same amount of service will *more than double* that of Sparseville. In the range of these two suburbs, at least, the relationship between density and ridership—if we give the two areas the same service—will be an upward curve.

It's a bit more complicated than that, but not much. Spillar and Rutherford[3] looked at several cities in the western United States and found that the relationship between density and transit demand has three distinct phases:

- In rural development, up to about 5 dwelling units per acre (12 units per hectare), demand is at a very low level, rising slowly in direct proportion to density.
- From 5 dwelling units per acre up to about 20 dwelling units per acre (50 units per hectare), demand rises faster than density, in the upward curve that we sketched above. This is the range in which most urban development in the New World occurs, outside of the densest urban cores. Both Denseville and Sparseville will be in this range, so this is the hard fact that governs how we apportion service between them.
- Above 20 dwelling units per acre, the steep curve starts to flatten out. At these high urban densities, people live so close to so many of their daily needs that walking trips begin to take a large share of the market at the expense of transit.

So the relationship between transit demand and residential density resembles that shown in figure 10-2.

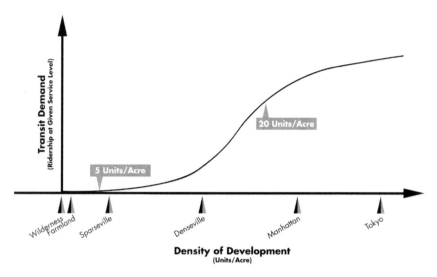

**Figure 10-2** How residential density affects transit demand. *Credit:* David Jones; adapted from Spillar and Rutherford, 1998

Most urban areas are made up of places like Denseville and Sparseville; they occupy the range of the density scale where the curve is upward. In other words, most of the time, *if you double the density, transit demand goes up by more than double.* Any workable policy for how to distribute service has to work with that reality.

## WHAT ABOUT JOB DENSITY?

Up to now, we have spoken of transit ridership as though it's generated only by residents. But of course, residences are only one end of most transit trips. The other end is some activity, such as a school, job, or shopping center. For simplicity, we have spoken of residential density. However, an effective service allocation policy will count both residential density and the density of activities that people need to travel to. In fact, the concentration of jobs seems to affect transit ridership even more profoundly than the concentration of residents. In the North American and Australasian context, this makes sense. Even in an era of car-oriented decentralization, high-rise

## What About Flexible Service?

Whenever I explain why Sparseville ridership is always lower than Denseville's, someone asks: "Would flexible or demand-responsive services do better in Sparseville?" The answer is: "Yes, sometimes, but not nearly enough to raise Sparseville ridership to Denseville levels." In both low-density suburban and rural areas, flexible services are a useful tool for optimizing performance and meeting hard-to-meet needs, but they don't let you avoid the service allocation question. For more, see http://www.humantransit.org/10box.html.

downtowns have remained important destinations, and the concentrations of jobs that they represent have been too intense to serve by private car. As a result, we have many data points about the transit impact of high-rise downtown employment, and they point to a strong relationship between the overall transit ridership in a region and the size of its high-rise downtown employment center(s).[4]

As employment spreads out, though, we need better ways of counting its impact on ridership, and also of counting the impact of other activities that can be more or less dense, such as shopping and other activities.

If we count density in terms of the number of *residents or jobs* per unit of area, we come close to describing density in the way it affects ridership. What we're really trying to count is what transport modelers call *trip generation* (how often does somebody in this zone want to go somewhere?) and *trip attraction* (how often does somebody want to go to somewhere in this zone?). Both are usually expressed in person trips generated or attracted, per day or per hour.

Trip generation and attraction is a hard thing to count, so we approximate. We count residents and jobs (and often student enrollments) because most governments know where those things are. We know that commutes to work and school are not the only trip purpose or even the most important one, but they are the easiest to measure.

Sometimes we try a more subtle analysis in which we weigh different kinds of jobs according to their ability to attract other trips besides the commute. For example, retail jobs represent a higher trip demand than manufacturing jobs, because for each person commuting to a retail job, there are many other people (customers) going to the same place. By contrast, a manufacturing job represents little or no additional demand, because few people visit factories apart from their employees.

Transport modeling is getting better, but very few governments have the data to completely describe all of our travel desires, and given our expectations for privacy as citizens, we probably wouldn't want them to. Counting residents plus jobs gives us a good rough approximation of where people want to go. Weighting jobs by their ability to attract noncommute trips would give us a better but more complicated approximation.

Let's stop there, because if we go too far into these details, we'll lose the big picture, which is defined by these two huge facts of geometry. First, *residential density is a major factor governing ridership*, and second, over the prevailing density range of our urban areas, *a doubling of residential density will more than double the transit demand*. Broadly speaking, these things are true of jobs and activities as well as housing, but to avoid the complexities of comparing the densities of these different destination types, I will continue to focus on residential density for the purposes of this chapter.

## FROM GEOMETRY TO POLICY

So given what we know about how density drives transit demand, how should a transit agency divide up its resources among the various communities that it serves? It depends entirely on what the goal of your transit system is. Let's recall again those two common goal statements that many agencies adopt:

Coverage: Serve all parts of our community.
Ridership: Maximize ridership with our fixed service budget.

Let's think about how you would actually deploy service to meet each of these goals.

## The Coverage Goal

If you're focused solely on a Coverage Goal, you run the same amount of service everywhere. If service is allocated this way, then residents will all enjoy the same frequency and span of service, no matter the density at which they live. The Coverage Goal is extreme, but it is quite common in smaller cities where transit is thought of primarily as a lifeline service for the dependent, not as a means of competing with the automobile.

Now, one problem of the Coverage Goal is obvious. Denseville is twice as dense as Sparseville, so we should expect it to produce *more than twice* the ridership. Let's assume that we'll get about three times the ridership in Denseville as in Sparseville. If the two communities have the same amount of service, then for every six people on the bus[d] in Sparseville, we should expect to see about 18 people on the bus in Denseville. If we get 15 people on the bus in Sparseville, then the buses in Denseville will be averaging 45 people, which usually means the seats are full and people are having to stand. When Denseville's loads pass 66 people and passengers start being left behind for lack of room, equivalent Sparseville buses will still have only 22 people on them, barely half a seated load.

Under the Coverage Goal, then, Sparseville residents complain about "all those empty buses." Meanwhile, Denseville transit riders complain of overcrowding and, even worse, of passengers being left behind.

On the surface, many people would agree with the principle of the Coverage Goal: that residents should all enjoy the same quality of service, regardless of the density at which they live. Someone who asks, "Why do they have good service and I don't?" is invoking a Coverage Goal.

But the Coverage Goal allocates service in proportion to *area*, not in proportion to *population*. Since Denseville has twice as many people, the Coverage Goal gives it only half as much service *per citizen*. We are only investing half as much in the mobility of a Denseville resident as in the mobility of a Sparseville resident. Is that a fair way to spend a public resource? When you put it that way, some people will say no.

---

[d] As often, I use the word *bus* here because there is no word for "transit vehicle of any technology." The references to overloading here assume a standard bus with around forty seats, but apart from that, this entire section is based on facts of geometry that are the same for buses, trains, streetcars, ferries, and so on.

## The Equity Goal: A Compromise?

To make the service fairer, then, we might propose an Equity Goal: "Service shall be allocated proportional to population." Under this goal, Denseville's transit line runs twice as frequently as Sparseville's. Perhaps the Sparseville bus runs every 30 minutes, whereas the Denseville bus runs every 15 minutes.

This may seem like the fairest arrangement. It's common to hear complaints about service allocation that presume an Equity Goal. For example, residents of an outer-suburban area may observe that they have the same population as a dense inner-city area that gets much more service. If you imply that population is the main yardstick for apportioning a public good, you're advocating an Equity Goal.

However, if we implement the Equity Goal, the buses in Denseville will still be more crowded. Under the Coverage Goal, Denseville's buses are three times as crowded as Sparseville's. Under the Equity Goal, Denseville gets twice as much service as Sparseville; now, its buses are still at least 1.5 times as crowded as those in Sparseville.

In fact, they're a bit more crowded than that, because in shifting from the Coverage Goal to the Equity Goal, we've now introduced a measurable difference in frequency. Denseville's buses are now twice as frequent as Sparseville's, and this frequency will attract more riders, again until we run into limits of capacity. So, Denseville's service will still be crowded, and sometimes overflowing.

The Equity Goal is fair in terms of the investment per citizen, but it will still draw complaints from all sides. Denseville residents will still find themselves standing, or even passed up, while Sparseville buses run with empty seats, which some residents will see as "our tax dollars going to waste." Meanwhile, it is hard to convince Sparseville residents that they're being treated fairly when they see buses in Denseville running twice as often. For this reason, it is often politically hard for a transit agency to implement even an Equity Goal.

## The Ridership Goal

But now, here come the environmentalists, demanding less traffic, cleaner air, and lower greenhouse gas emissions. They ask a different question: Are we allocating transit resources to carry as many riders as possible within our budget? They want to get cars off the road, and the near-empty buses driving around Sparseville are obviously not doing that, or not very efficiently.

From another direction, here come the fiscal conservatives, who would prefer that transit either run at a profit or not run at all. At the very least, they want transit to run with the lowest possible subsidy per passenger. Their question turns out to be the same as that of the environmentalist: Are we allocating transit resources to carry as many riders as possible within our budget? The environmentalist thinks of riders as cars off the road rather than as revenue, but the basic question is the same.

Even under the Equity Goal, the answer is clearly no. If the goal is to carry as many passengers as possible, we should cut service further in Sparseville, where there are still empty seats, and add service in Denseville, where our overcrowded buses are pushing customers away.

Think about it another way: if we cut an hour of bus service in Sparseville, where it carried, say, ten people, and add that hour of service in Denseville, where it may carry thirty people, then the ridership of our transit system goes up, even though the cost of running the service is the same. To anyone preoccupied with getting cars off the road, that seems like a good deal. Fiscal conservatives who want higher fare revenue will like it too. That's what the Ridership Goal does: it deploys service wherever it will carry the most people, even if that means cutting service to some Sparsevilles entirely.[e]

Figure 10-3 shows the three strategies conceptually:

- The Coverage Goal apportions service regardless of density. (Denseville and Sparseville get the same service.)
- The Equity Goal apportions service proportional to density. (Denseville gets twice as much service as Sparseville because it has twice the population.)
- The Ridership Goal apportions service in response to the observed pattern of demand. (Denseville generates more than twice as much demand as Sparseville, so it gets more than twice as much service.)

---

[e] In practice, a network designed to a Ridership Goal may serve Sparseville via a large park-and-ride nearby, which allows Sparseville residents to gather at one stop so that they can be served efficiently. Service that circulates through Sparseville, however, is rarely justified by a Ridership Goal.

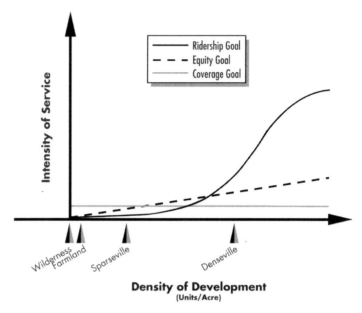

**Figure 10-3**   Three service allocation goals. *Source:* David Jones

The choice among these goals is the purest of value judgments, a plumber's question. There's no right or wrong answer. It depends on why you're running public transit at all.

## FROM POLICY TO NETWORK

How would the different policies affect the design of a network? Figure 10-4 shows the extremes of an all-Coverage and all-Ridership network for a fictional town with uneven distributions of density.

Given twelve all-day buses to deploy, the Coverage network would provide service on almost every operable street. To do this, it would need eight lines, so with twelve buses it could run two buses on four of these lines, but the rest would have only one bus—a very poor frequency.

At the opposite extreme, a Ridership-oriented network would focus all service where density—and, hence, ridership potential—is highest. This

Here's a transit agency's service area. The lines are roads, and the small people indicate population density. The agency can deploy twelve buses.

## RIDERSHIP GOAL

For ridership, concentrate all service in denser areas. Three lines each have 4 vehicles, offering frequent service.

## COVERAGE GOAL

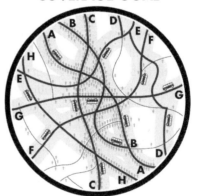

For coverage, you need eight routes, so each will have only 1-2 vehicles, offering infrequent service.

**Figure 10-4** Extreme service allocation goals in a fictional city. *Credit:* David Jones

system would need just three lines, but each line could have four buses on it. The Ridership network would run the fewest possible lines, so as to support the highest possible frequency.

This is a small-city local example where the demand is mostly all-day. In other situations, a Ridership-oriented network might have other service types. For example, in a suburban commuter market that is highly peaked (see chapter 6), the Ridership-oriented network might run lots of commuter express service—bus, rail, or ferry—with a heavily peaked service pattern and little or no midday service.

## ANSWERING THE PLUMBER'S QUESTION: SERVICE ALLOCATION POLICIES

Often, when working with elected officials governing transit systems, I try to develop consensus around a *Service Allocation Policy*, which takes the form of a percentage split of resources between the different goals. For example, an agency might decide to allocate 55 percent of its service according to the Ridership Goal and 45 percent according to the Coverage Goal.

With that direction, the transit planners are finally given a coherent assignment. They can design services to meet those goals, document which services are which, and monitor the results. For example, services justified by the Ridership Goal would be assessed based on their ridership, whereas services justified by the Coverage Goal would be assessed based on the percentage of the population that they cover and the efficiency with which they do that.

The transit agency in greater Reno, Nevada, for example, has used this approach since 2005. The long-range planning document, the Regional Transportation Plan, states a long-term intention to reach a certain percentage split between Ridership and Coverage Goals. That split was adopted by the elected officials who govern the agency, after public discussion. When planners propose a short-term service change, they must show how it moves the system toward that intention.[5]

A wider use of this approach would also blunt much of the confusion that arises from total performance figures for an entire system. Anti-transit advocates often cite the low overall productivity of a network as evidence of transit's failure.[6] In fact, they should look only at the services where Ridership is the goal. Coverage services are not trying to be highly productive, so they're not failing if they aren't. Average productivity for a whole system can confuse these issues.

Obviously, not every elected official is comfortable making this decision in terms of abstract percentages. It's not hard, though, to draw some sample network plans for a city that will help people see what each goal would mean. For example, when helping a transit agency think through a long-term network plan, I'll often present two or more alternative networks that have the same operating cost but differ in the balance between Coverage-justified services and Ridership-justified services. If I explain that this option is, say, 40 percent Coverage and 60 percent Ridership, while this other option is the opposite, people can see what the numbers mean in real life and can "vote" for a particular split between Coverage and Ridership that matches their own priorities. Those votes constitute public guidance that can actually be followed, because the guidance addresses an actual question that transit agencies face.

But no agency should pretend to be meeting both Coverage and Ridership goals with the same dollar. Consciously or not, every transit agency is making a choice about how to balance these competing goals. By stating the choice explicitly, and triggering a clear public debate about it, a Service Allocation Policy process can yield a more informed and durable consensus.

## THE FEEDBACK LOOP: DENSITY, SERVICE, AND RIDERSHIP

Before we leave Denseville and Sparseville, we should be clearer about why so many sustainability advocates want to build more Densevilles, and the role transit can play in helping to do that.

The high-quality transit in Denseville—especially if it's readily visible via tools like a Frequent Network map (chapter 7)—can make more people want to locate there. If your city's politicians and developers allow that to happen, Denseville will get even denser. Now you have a feedback loop, because density, service, and ridership are all feeding off of one another, each growing because the other two are growing. That path can lead to denser and also much more sustainable cities, where transit plays a huge role in mobility while walking and cycling, supplemented by carsharing, do much of the rest.

As this happens, each Sparseville needs to decide whether to become a little denser, and so take on some of these benefits, or to protect its car-oriented low density. Again, there isn't a right answer. If a Sparseville wants to become more like Denseville, then it too can be the site of a positive feedback loop that benefits the whole city's environmental outcomes, so it makes sense for the whole city to help it do that. On the other hand, if a Sparseville chooses to protect its low densities and large lots, it will remain a car-dependent place. That isn't a problem for transit's performance, so long as Sparseville doesn't demand too much low-ridership service.

But while there are larger environmental reasons to worry about car dependence, Sparseville isn't the place to do it, because for people in Sparseville, relying on cars for most travel is the rational thing to do. If the goal is to drive down car ownership and car dependence for environmental reasons, the best place to do that is in Denseville, and in those Sparsevilles that choose to become more like Denseville, because there, the feedback loop of service, ridership, and density is something that the political process can build on. As an area gets denser and fewer people own cars, it becomes possible to change many of the policies that get in the way of creating great urban places—policies around parking supply, for example, as well as zoning. Transit will be helping to build the city.

# 11

# CAN FARES BE FAIR?

Fares are a tough issue for transit agencies and the politicians they answer to. If you see transit ridership as a benefit to the entire community (for either social or environmental reasons), then you want fares to be low, or even eliminated entirely. Right now, though, the financial bottom line of most agencies requires a certain level of fare revenue, and people focused on reducing the scope of government will want that level to be higher.

## TRANSIT SUBSIDIES VERSUS CAR SUBSIDIES

Most transit agencies worry about their "farebox return," which is the percentage of operating cost paid for by fares. If it's more than 100 percent, you have a profitable business, but in the developed world it's usually much less. For that reason, transit in wealthy countries relies on government subsidies, which must be justified based on transit's benefit to the community as a whole, not just to its riders.

A similar calculation can be made for private cars. While transit riders pay fares, motorists pay a range of fees or taxes tied directly to their driving (distinct from other taxes that people pay as citizens). All motorists pay for vehicle registration and taxes added to the cost of fuel. Some urban motorists also pay tolls or congestion charges to use high-demand facilities. All of those charges add up to the total "user fee" of driving, just as fares are the user fee of transit. If the true costs of a mode exceed the user fees collected for it, that mode is being subsidized, usually by taxpayers in general, and in that case it is fair to ask why.

Since transit and cars compete for customers, the fares and other user fees can tilt the playing field of that competition, giving an advantage to one side. So it's important to ask two questions. First, is the playing field level now? Do cars and transit get comparable levels of subsidy? Second, *should* the playing field be level, or should it be tilted to favor a mode that produces greater social and environmental benefit?

Transit opponents and road advocates often argue that the playing field is tilted toward transit.[1] They claim that fuel taxes (the motorist's equivalent of transit fares) pay for roads, while transit relies on subsidy from all taxpayers. Road construction and maintenance, however, is only one of the costs of motoring. There are many other costs, most of them effectively hidden from the motorist and subsidized in other ways.

Parking, for example, consumes vast amounts of expensive land but is usually offered free, or at costs far below the fair rental value of the real estate. For housing, parking costs are typically hidden in the cost of the housing unit, so that residents must pay for the parking even if they don't use it. For shopping destinations, the cost of parking is considered a basic cost of doing business, so it's hidden in the prices the customer pays. For employment destinations, free parking is an expensive benefit to certain employees but not to others. The work of making these subsidies visible, and accounting for them fairly, is only just beginning. The definitive study of the problem is Donald Shoup's book *The High Cost of Free Parking*.[2]

Cars also impose negative impacts that are not connected directly to user costs paid by motorists. These include public health impacts (obesity, accident rates), several kinds of pollution, greenhouse gas emissions, and runoff from the hard surfaces of roads and parking lots. They also include oil dependence, which is an environmental problem (oil spills and other kinds of production-related damage) and also a foreign policy problem (the need to influence the politics of oil-rich countries).[3]

For most people, cars are so completely imbedded in the fabric of life that these costs are hard to talk about, so any discussion of this issue arouses defensiveness. Now and then, you'll hear dark talk about a "war on motorists." But the costs that cars impose on society and the environment are real. As long as those costs are hidden, transit advocates should not be ashamed about requiring subsidies, or about advocating even larger subsidies, because of the clear benefits of transit to the community.

I have not dwelled much on these benefits, because many publications cover the issue. In general, transit allows growth in economic activity without growth in congestion. It allows a city's economy, and hence its employment, to grow beyond the level where road congestion would otherwise cap it. Transit also meets important social service needs and permits the development of more compact and sustainable communities in places where that is desired. The government subsidy of transit—which allows lower fares and thus higher ridership—directly purchases all of these benefits.

## SHOULD FARES BE FREE?

If we ever really accounted for all the invisible subsidies to the motorist, and set transit subsidies to fairly balance those subsidies, we would see huge growth in transit funding, which might make it possible to eliminate fares. It's worth noting, however, that even in countries with very high levels of government activity and environmental commitment—such as those of northern Europe—no big-city transit agency has done this yet.

Currently, free fares can be found in three specialized situations:

- Rural and small-city systems where ridership is so low that the fares don't even pay for the cost of collecting fares. Several rural and small-city agencies in the State of Washington have eliminated fares, as has the Logan area of Utah.[4]
- Small cities with big universities, where university-sponsored student ridership dominates. Universities seeking to improve their own sustainability profile, and to reduce the need for expensive on-campus parking, often discover that subsidizing student transit fares makes financial sense for them. In small cities—including Hasselt, Belgium, and Chapel Hill, North Carolina—these subsidized riders may be 80 percent or more of the total system ridership. At that point, it's easier for all concerned to stop charging fares and treat the university's subsidy as the agency's entire fare revenue.

- Downtown circulation. If a city government is focused on revitalizing or reducing congestion downtown and the transit agency has surplus capacity there, it can make sense to make fares free just for travel around downtown, as a way to motivate downtown commuters and visitors to leave their cars at home. Many cities have a separate system of free downtown shuttles. Others offer free service just on the downtown segments of its regular lines.

Why can't we make all fares free in big cities, causing a potentially huge shift toward public transit? The short-term answer is that big-city systems are already crowded at least during the peak period and simply wouldn't have the capacity to handle all the riders that free fares would attract. As we saw in chapter 6, rush-hour service is expensive, because it requires short driver shifts and raises the fleet size. Even if a big-city agency could afford the loss of revenue, the sudden influx of service that would be required is far beyond the budget reality of any big-city transit agency today. These calculations could change as policy priorities change, and especially if car subsidies are made more visible, but as of this writing in 2011, no big-city transit systems are completely or even mostly fare-free.

## FARE STRUCTURE: THE HARD QUESTIONS

Transit agencies that set fares have to answer some difficult questions:

- Should people pay more to travel farther? If so, how do we keep track of this?
- Should people pay extra if their trip requires a connection?
- Should there be "frequent rider discounts," such as a reduced price for tickets bought in bulk or a discounted "pass" for unlimited rides in a day, a week, a month, or a year?
- Should there be discounts for using the service only at times when it has spare capacity, such as outside the peak commute period?

All of these issues are matters of active debate, and you will see a wide range of policies from one city or agency to the next. In North America, where transit is especially decentralized, you may even see multiple policies in the same urban area.

## WHAT SMARTCARDS DO

The transit industry is in transition to a new fare collection technology, generally called a smartcard. Smartcards have different brand names in different cities, and their exact capabilities vary. In general, though, a smartcard is a plastic card that stores some of your money and enables you to spend it by simply swiping the card against a reader. In principle, it works just like a bank debit card, except that you don't have to enter a personal identification number (PIN) or sign anything. Just wave the card at a reader, and the transaction occurs. Your fare is removed from your account.

For a typical middle-income people who don't have to count every penny they are spending, smartcards offer liberation from fare complexity. Arcane fare systems can impose huge and unnecessary hassle on all riders. In Sydney, Australia, for example, an occasional rider has to choose from among three types of single-ride fare on buses, to be used for trips of different lengths, and needs yet another ticket, with a different system of distance charges, to connect to trains or ferries.[5] (The system was rebranded in 2010 but without fixing any of these problems.) To many people, the money involved is minor, but the sheer complexity is enough to make them give up on transit.

Smartcards sweep away all the hassle. Just ride where and when you want. Swipe your card as you board, and sometimes also when you get off, and the card will figure out your fare and debit your account.

This capability of smartcards isn't new. There have long been magnetic-stripe tickets that can store value and deduct it, but unfortunately, many urban regions haven't seen a consistent adoption of those tickets. For example, the San Francisco Bay Area's BART rapid transit system has used stored-value magnetic strip tickets since it opened in 1972, but the connecting bus, ferry, and light rail agencies each had their own ticketing systems that weren't compatible with it. Only now is a smartcard being introduced that will work on all of the Bay Area's transit systems.

The new plastic smartcard has several additional features:

* It is generally "contactless," which means it can just be waved next to a sensor rather than being slid into a mechanical reader. This difference can substantially speed up boarding and alighting time.

- Smartcard systems can be programmed to run a wide variety of fare structures and policies.
- Smartcards are being implemented across entire urban regions so will generally be useful on all transit services in a city, even if those services are run by different agencies with different fare structures.
- Smartcards can keep track of connections that ordinary magnetic-stripe tickets don't. When you board a transit vehicle, the smartcard knows whether you just got off of a different vehicle, so it can calculate whether you should have a discount, or whether you shouldn't be charged at all, depending on the connection policy of the agency.
- Smartcards know where they are because they're connected to systems that keep track of the vehicle's location. This means that smartcards can keep track of distance-based fares, even ones that keep track of small increments of distance, like Sydney's. They can also produce a rich mine of data about how the transit system is being used, enabling planners to make smarter choices about network design and to respond more rapidly to issues.[a]

As always with new technology, it's tempting to imagine that smartcards will make the problems of fare policy go away. They won't. Communities and their transit agencies still need to think about fares. Three questions are especially interesting. Should we discount fares to use spare capacity? Should fares vary by distance? Should connections be free?

## SHOULD FARES BE FREE OR DISCOUNTED OUTSIDE THE PEAK?

What if fares were free or reduced outside the peak period, when transit agencies have empty seats? Seattle's King County Metro has long done this, charging $0.25 less outside the peak when their service has spare ca-

---

[a] It can be very hard to get data on ridership on a stop-by-stop basis, especially on bus systems. Until recently, this could be done only by an expensive manual survey (people with clipboards on each bus, counting passengers at each stop). This data is crucial if you want to redesign a network intelligently, because it shows exactly how many existing riders are affected (for better or for worse) by any proposed routing change. Smartcards should provide a sudden feast of detailed information, which should lead to a flurry of much more effective network redesigns.

pacity.[6] Melbourne, Australia, has free train fares if you board very early in the morning, before 7:00 a.m., when trains aren't yet full.[7] Some agencies eliminate senior discounts during the peak period, on the theory that retired people have more flexibility about when they travel and should therefore be encouraged to travel at less crowded times. As we saw in chapter 6, peak capacity is expensive to provide, so it's reasonable to charge more for it.

Until now, the main objection to off-peak discounts has been complexity. Transit agencies must keep track of discounts in several dimensions, often including connections, distance-based fares, express fares, and senior-disabled discounts, so discounting off-peak service has been considered just too complicated. Smartcards will eliminate that problem. In some cases, midday and evening discounts might actually increase ridership enough so that total fare revenue is constant.

## TIME-BASED OR DISTANCE-BASED FARES?

When you pay a fare, you get a ticket to ride some distance, usually also limited by a period of time. Distance may be calculated using either fare zones or very small units such as fare sections, typically about a mile long. Distance-based fares can get very complicated, and this complexity itself discourages ridership. So, some agencies try to minimize distance factors and think of the fare as a ticket to ride for a duration of time. For example, many cities have distance-based fare zones for their suburbs but treat the whole central city as a single zone. Within that zone, where most tourists and visitors stay, a ticket entitles you to one ride, and maybe a connection, but expires in 1 to 2 hours.

Smartcards handle all of this complexity and allow more innovation in how fares are constructed using mixtures of distance-based and time-based elements.

## FARES AND CONNECTIONS

An especially awkward fare issue arises around connections, which we'll explore in chapter 12. Connections are an integral part of any transit system that aims for maximum frequency and simplicity—the sort of system that you can remember, at least in its outlines, as you move freely around your city.

From this point of view, connections should be free. The connection is not an added product or service; rather, it's an inconvenience imposed on the customer by the geometry of the transit system. Transit agencies can't eliminate this inconvenience but they can certainly avoid adding to it by including a free connection in any fare.

Unfortunately, there have been many practical problems with free connections, depending on how agencies keep track of them. The typical North American tool was a "transfer slip," a little piece of paper given out in return for your original fare, which would permit you to board a second or third bus or train to complete your journey. These transfer slips have always been sources of trouble. People who don't need them sell them or give them away, causing significant losses in fare revenue. In the United States, some agencies have eliminated free connections and instead offer a day pass at around twice the base fare. This approach still penalizes customers who are making spontaneous one-way trips, and these customers are a very important part of the life of the city.

The advent of smartcards will eliminate the practical problems surrounding connection penalties, making it easy to offer free connections without encouraging fraud. Of course, any fare reduction, even this one, has a short-term downward effect on fare revenue, so it may not be politically painless. But I have never heard a theoretical justification for why a transit system should penalize connections. Airlines certainly don't do it; in fact, itineraries that require a connection are sometimes cheaper than direct flights. It will be interesting to see how quickly connection penalties disappear as smartcards become the norm.

## BEYOND FAIR FARES?

After dealing with these issues for years as a consultant, I'm beginning to suspect that we might do well to set aside the idea of "fairness" or "equity" in fares. When we're talking about fares, everyone wants (a) to pay less and (b) to perceive that the system is fair or equitable. But a simple thought experiment should tell us that we don't really want fairness at all.

Suppose that in our perfect transit system, a fare policy really did charge everyone for exactly their fair share of the cost of providing the service that they use. If you really wanted to do that, you'd do exactly what you'd do if you and a few other people were sharing a ride in a private vehicle. You'd want everyone to pay the cost of running the trip *divided by the number of people riding.*

Clearly, your fare would depend on the distance you travel, but it would depend much more dramatically on the number of other passengers on your bus, train, or ferry. If you were the only passenger on a forty-seat bus, your fare would be forty times higher than if every seat was filled. Your fare would be calculated in tiny increments extending from one bus stop or train station to the next. As the bus or train filled up, the increments would get cheaper. As it emptied out, their cost would go up. The sum of all these increments is what you'd pay for the trip.[b]

As fare technology continues to develop, it is not hard to imagine a future "very smart card" system that could actually calculate this "perfectly equitable fare" in real time. It would know not just where you started and ended your trip but also how many other smartcards were on the same vehicle with you. At the end of your trip, it would debit your card for the cost of each increment of the trip, divided by the number of people who used that increment. This system, and only this system, could be called "equitable" in the sense that everyone, at every moment, would be paying exactly his or her fair share of the costs of running the service.

Obviously, no transit agency does anything like this, and I have yet to see it seriously proposed even for the new era of smartcards. I don't propose it myself, but I do think it's a valid representation of fairness on an analogy to the way people split costs "fairly" among themselves when sharing some other good, whether it's a taxi ride, a dinner at a restaurant, or the fuel costs of a car trip they take together.

---

[b] Such a system would need many refinements to capture the subtleties of cost and market. For example, we know that on most services, the last scheduled trip of the night isn't full, but that if we delete it, ridership on the preceding trip (now the last) often drops suddenly. People's decision to use transit appears to be influenced by the availability of trips later than the one they use—presumably because later trips offer some reassurance that you won't be stranded if late. So, the costs of these later trips would need to be spread over some of the earlier trips, to capture this interdependence.

As a practical policy, it would have some dramatic consequences. People would stop cursing the transit agency for not giving everyone a seat during rush hour. Instead, they would actively try to pack themselves onto already-crowded buses and trains. At the other extreme, low-ridership services would become prohibitively expensive to ride. For better or for worse, the policy would certainly yield a very high-ridership transit system, because high-ridership service would be the only service most people could afford to use. But it would all be perfectly fair, wouldn't it?

This thought experiment tells us several important things:

- Equity begets complexity. The more precisely equitable a fare system tries to be, the more complicated it becomes. For example, cities that charge for very small units of distance have much more complicated fares than cities that charge a the same fare everywhere (a *flat fare*) or have just a few fare zones. Our "perfectly equitable fare" achieves the extreme of complexity: it is so intricate that when they set out, nobody can know what the fare will turn out to be.

- Complexity for the passenger is different from complexity for the agency, largely thanks to smartcards. Until the advent of smartcards, agencies and their customers had a shared interest in fare simplicity, because a system that was too complex for customers to understand was usually also too complex to administer and enforce. Smartcards now make it possible to administer and enforce extremely complex fare systems. This does not necessarily mean that we should welcome these systems, because of the following point.

- Fare complexity will still be a problem for people who need to know their fare in advance. Some customers have enough financial security that they don't need to worry about small increments of cost; for such a customer, the hassle of figuring out complicated fares and tickets is a much bigger ridership deterrent than the amounts of money involved. Smartcards will liberate this passenger from that hassle, regardless of the fare system used. However, some passengers will always need the ability to predict what they will spend. Others may not need this ability but will insist that they have a right to it. Fare complexity will continue to weigh primarily on these customers, and if the agency chooses to continue to value simplicity in its fare structure, it is these customers who will benefit.

Equity in the sense of "fair share of cost" is clearly related to how many people are using a given service, yet this enormous factor is almost never expressed in conventional fares. It can be crudely approximated, for example, by charging more for services that carry few passengers by design, such as services designed to serve a Coverage Goal, but this is rarely done in current fare practice. As noted above, with each such factor, we increase the equity of a fare structure but also increase its complexity.

Once we consider this "fair share of cost" system, it becomes clear that any real-world fare system is an extremely crude approximation of equity. Thus, any transit agency that is unprepared to implement "perfectly equitable" fares, as described above, must accept being accused of inequity as an inevitable consequence of whatever decision it makes. This does not mean that the decision is unimportant or can be taken lightly, but only that we shouldn't expect to achieve "equity" or "fairness" in any measurable sense.

The real purpose of a fare system is to bring in a needed level of revenue while imposing a minimum of delay, hassle, confusion, and perverse incentives. Effective fare systems focus on these outcomes, support the goals of the network design, and accept that they will never be perfectly fair.

# 12

# CONNECTIONS OR COMPLEXITY?

When using any type of passenger transport service, you sometimes have to make a *connection*, which means to get off of one vehicle and get on another. You take a train to a station and then catch a local bus. You catch a ferry to the downtown dock but then need a bus to get up the hill to where you're going. Or, you may have to connect within the same mode: from one bus to another, or from one train to another.

Airlines often require connections too, especially to travel between smaller cities. Airlines usually have hubs, a handful of airports (often just one) where all of their flights begin or end. If you're at one of these hubs, you can fly nonstop to destinations all over the airline's network. If you aren't, you'll probably have to fly to one of these hubs and make a connection. These hubs exist because the airlines want to connect a lot of cities and make it possible to fly between any pair of those cities. To do that, flights to and from many cities have to come together at the same airport, so that you can connect between any flight and any other.

As every airline, train company, and transit agency knows, you don't *want* to make a connection. What you really want is direct service to where you're going. And if you have such a service now and I take it away and require you to make a connection instead, you're going to be mad at me.

Still, if a transit agency wants me to do a network plan that will increase its ridership and efficiency, I almost always have to delete some direct services and introduce connections. This chapter is about why, and about the great things you can achieve only if you accept the need to change vehicles in the course of your trip.

In the end, embracing connections is a values trade-off, a plumber's question. If avoiding connections is important enough to you, you can design a network that does that. But understand what you sacrifice by doing so.

## THE RARE MANY-TO-ONE NETWORK

Connection-free networks can work well in one instance: where absolutely everyone is going to the same destination. Such networks are called *many-to-one*, because their purpose is to link many places where people live to a single place where, we assume, everyone is going. They're also called *radial*, because all lines extend from a single point. Of course, a radial network is just like an airline hub network but with the primary intention of serving the hub city rather than encouraging connections among other city pairs.

We sometimes imagine a long-lost idealized city in which everybody commuted to downtown, and all of downtown was small enough to be in walking distance of a few transit stops. In such cities, all transit networks were simple many-to-one networks, where all the lines radiated out from downtown. Everyone had direct service to where they were going because everyone (who mattered)[a] was going to the same place. If they weren't going there, they'd have to make a connection there.

Regardless of the shape of your city, you can still do a radial network; all you have to do is narrow your focus and decide that only one destination matters. If you do have a really dominant downtown and few other destinations of importance, a radial network may be a decent approximation of what your community needs. If you're a small town with a big university, you may well want a network that radiates from the university, because most of your riders are going there.

Of course, you may also be running a specialized network built around a single destination: an airport shuttle system, say, or a network of commuter buses funded by a single employer to get people to a single suburban office park. In these cases, radial systems make perfect sense, and connections, if any, play a smaller role.

---

[a] Even in the most single-centered cities, it was never true that everyone was going downtown. But an influential segment of the population, the middle-class commuter, would only consider transit for that purpose, because only downtown offered a reason not to drive—typically, congestion and parking costs.

Finally, as we saw in chapter 3, a few cities are one-dimensional, with most travel demand along a single path. Beach towns can often have this shape, because they grow along the beach but not so much inland. In that rare case, you can run a single line connecting all the important markets, and not require connections.

But if you're a transit system serving an typical city, with many centers of activity that people want to get to, you have a *many-to-many* demand pattern. At this point, you face a plumber's question: connections or complexity? If you try to serve a many-to-many demand pattern but try to avoid connections, you'll produce a network that's massively complex and much less frequent than it could otherwise be.

## CONNECTIONS BUY FREQUENCY

Imagine a simple city that has three primary residential areas (shown along the top in figure 12-1) and three primary areas of employment or activity

**Figure 12-1** A simple city: three residential areas, three activity centers. *Credit:* Alfred Twu

(shown along the bottom). In designing a network for this city, the first impulse is to try to run direct service from each residential area to each activity center. If we have three of each, this yields a network of nine transit lines (figure 12-2a). Suppose that we can afford to run each line every 30 minutes. Call this the *Direct Service Option*.

Now consider another way of serving this simple city for the same cost (figure 12-2b). Instead of running a direct line between every residential area and every activity center, we run a direct line from each residential area to *one* activity center, but we make sure that all the resulting lines connect with one another at a strategic point.

Now we have three lines instead of nine, so we can run each line three times as often at the same total cost as the Direct Service Option. So instead of service every 30 minutes, we have service every 10 minutes. Let's call this the *Connective Option*.

Without increasing operating cost, we've tripled the frequency of service, which has many profound benefits in terms of attracting ridership:

- A 10-minute frequency approaches a level of service where people stop worrying about a timetable and think of the service as being there whenever they need it. This is the critical psychological shift, where transit starts to become useful for people who value freedom.
- Frequency also means you're less dependent on the reliability of any one trip, because even if a vehicle breaks down or runs late, you'll still have another service soon.
- Finally, even though the Connective Option forces you to wait for a connection, your total trip time is likely to be faster.

Let's look at that last point, because few people believe it until they see it.

In figure 12-2, look at trips from Neighborhood 1 to the College. For simplicity, let's also assume that all the lines, in all the scenarios, are 20 minutes long. Table 12-1 compares the average travel times in each scenario.

In the Direct Service scenario (figure 12-2a), a service runs directly from Neighborhood 1 to the College. It runs every 30 minutes, so the average waiting time is 15 minutes. Once we're onboard, the travel time is 20 minutes. So, the average trip time is 35 minutes.

**a)**

# Direct Service Option

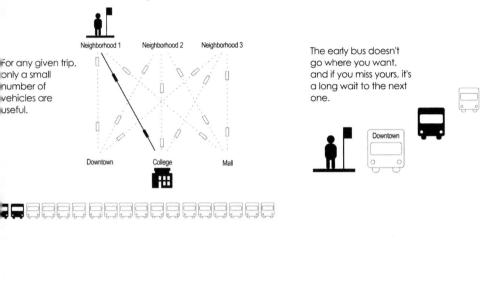

For any given trip, only a small number of vehicles are useful.

The early bus doesn't go where you want, and if you miss yours, it's a long wait to the next one.

**b)**

# Connective Option

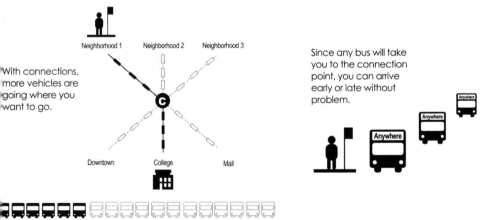

With connections, more vehicles are going where you want to go.

Since any bus will take you to the connection point, you can arrive early or late without problem.

**Figure 12-2** Two ways of serving the simple city. *Credit:* Alfred Twu

**Table 12-1** Total Average Travel Time, Neighborhood 1 to College (per figure 12-2)

| Direct Service Option | | | Connective Option | |
|---|---|---|---|---|
| Wait | 15 min | | Wait | 5 min |
| Ride | 20 min | | Ride | 10 min |
| | | | Connection Wait | 5 min |
| | | | Ride | 10 min |
| Total Trip Time | 35 min | Total Trip Time | | 30 min |

Now look at the Connective Option (figure 12-2b). We leave Neighborhood 1 on its only line. It runs every 10 minutes, so our average wait is 5 minutes. We ride to the connection point and get off. Since this point is halfway between the neighborhoods and the activity centers, the travel time to it is 10 minutes. Now we get off and wait for the service to the College. It also runs every 10 minutes, so our average wait time is 5 minutes. Finally, our ride from the connection point to the College is 10 minutes. So, our average trip time is 30 minutes. The Connective network gets us to our destination faster, even though it imposes a connection, because of the much higher frequencies that it can offer for the same total budget.

In inferring an average wait time from the frequency, I'm assuming that you want to go whenever you want to go and that you have not organized your life around the transit schedule. Commuter express services assume that people do organize their lives around the schedule. If you take the 5:15 p.m. bus home every day, you don't care about what the frequency is, and you don't wait long, because you've already planned your trip around when the service runs. That's why commuter express services tend to be much less connective.

As cities grow, the travel time advantages of the Connective Option increase. For example, suppose that instead of having three residential areas and three activity centers, we had six of each. In this case, the Direct Service Option would have thirty-six routes whereas the Connective Option would have only six. You can run the numbers yourself, but the answer is that the Direct Service Option still takes 35 minutes, while the Connective

## The Words I'm Not Using

Why am I not using the common American words *transfer* and *transferring*? I'm not using them because they may have unfortunate connotations. See www.humantransit.org/12box.html.

Option is down to only 25 minutes, because each line can now run every 5 minutes in the Connective Option.

The geometry at work here is exactly the same for buses, trains, and even ferries. Look again at the Direct Service and Connective Options in figure 12-2. They're drawn with buses, but instead of roads, you could imagine that there are tracks and rail stations. You can even imagine the middle of the map as water, and the upper and lower sides of the map as ferry terminals serving each community. In that case, if you had an island in the middle of the drawing, you could still run the Connective Option via a stop on that island.

## CONNECTIONS FREE US FROM COMPLEXITY

Even in the simplified abstract city that I've used in this example, the Connective network has one more crucial advantage: it's simpler. It has three lines instead of nine, so you can learn the whole system with only a third as much effort. That's important if you want to move around your city spontaneously on transit, as opposed to just making one regular trip.

Of course, this abstract city is so simple that the difference hardly matters, but as the city gets bigger, the benefits of a Connective network get bigger too. Figures 12-3 and 12-4 show a slice of the all-day transit network of Sydney, Australia, and a slice of San Francisco. Both are taken from an area just south of downtown. Both show an area about 5 miles (8 km) wide and 2 miles (3 km) high.

Sydney, Australia, has an exceptionally complicated bus system. For example, suppose you want to get from Taylor Square on the inner east side

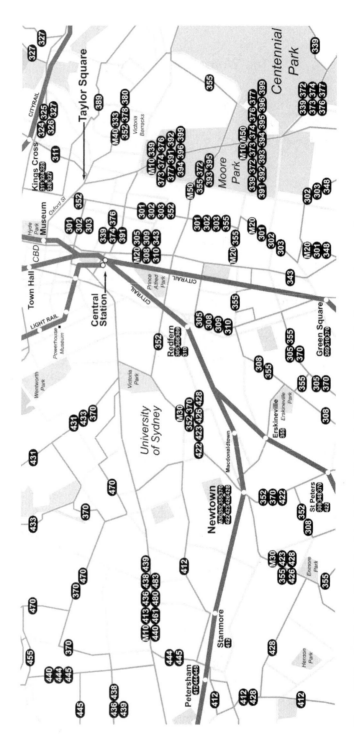

**Figure 12-3** A 5- by 2-mile (8- by 3-km) slice of Sydney's all-day network. *Credit*: Daniel Howard

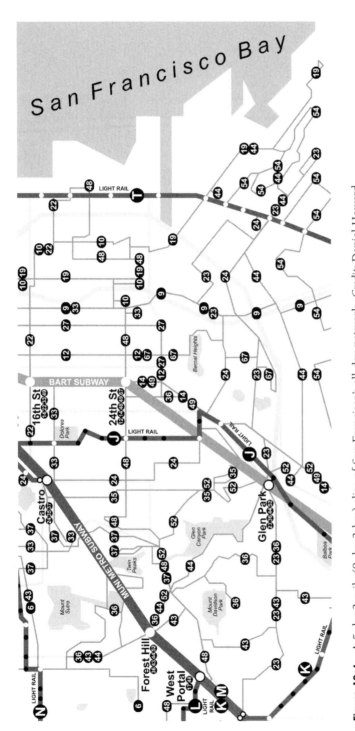

**Figure 12-4** A 5- by 2-mile (8- by 3-km) slice of San Francisco's all-day network. *Credit:* Daniel Howard

of Sydney to the Newtown district in the inner west. Here's what you need to know:[1]

> There's a direct bus from Taylor Square to Newtown, the 352, but it only runs until 7:00 PM and it only runs every 30 minutes. If you've just missed the 352, or it's not running, you'll need to take a bus into the central city and then another bus or train to Newtown. To get to the central city you go to an inbound stop on Oxford Street and take the M10, M40, 333, 373, 377, 380, 392, 394, 396 or 399, but not the 311 or 378.* Then you go to Castlereagh Street and catch bus M30 or any bus numbered in the 420s, or you can take an Inner West line train from Town Hall station.

For a trip between two of the busiest nodes in inner-city Sydney, a straight-line distance of only 2.3 miles (3.7 km), that's a lot of complexity. I chose Taylor Square and Newtown for this example because both are very transit-oriented places, dense mixtures of housing, offices, shopping, and nightlife. Both have very limited parking. Both have many resources pitched to younger adults, who are less likely to be able to afford the high costs of keeping a car in Sydney. Both have major hospitals nearby, and Newtown is also the main commercial district serving the University of Sydney. In short, these are both areas where lots of people are coming and going all day, people who already have good reasons not to use cars, so you should expect a high demand for transit. Yet, the network is so complicated that this basic trip is remarkably hard to make, and even harder to remember.

How is it different in San Francisco? Again, let's pick two nightlife districts with vibrant activity all day and all evening, the Marina district (near the north end of Fillmore Street) and the Castro district, centered on Castro rail station. It's about the same distance as our sample Sydney trip. (It's not on the slice of San Francisco in figure 12-4, so figure 12-5 shows the lines involved.) Here are your transit directions:

---

* However if the 311 or 378 comes first, take it. In that case you'll end up at Railway Square on the west side of Central Station, and you can catch the M30, or any of the 420s, to Newtown from there.

**Figure 12-5** A trip from the Marina district to the Castro district, San Francisco. *Source:* Daniel Howard

Take Line 22 south to Church Station, then take any outbound train in the Muni Metro subway (K, L, or M), or surface streetcar F.

Pretty simple. There's a little Sydney-like complexity in "K, L, or M," but you don't even have to remember that, because you can take any line that's in the subway at that point. The surface streetcar is an option only because the second part of your trip is very short, just under one half mile

(0.8 km), so while the streetcar is slower than the subway, it's faster for you if you happen to see it coming, because you save the 2 to 3 minutes it will take to get into and out of the subway.

Note that San Francisco's Fillmore Street has only one bus line on it. In Sydney, a street with only one bus line is usually a pretty unimportant street; the sign of "majorness" in Sydney's bus network is a huge and confusing pile of line numbers. But San Francisco's Line 22-Fillmore is major all by itself. For most of the day, it runs every 5 minutes, and even late into the evening it's every 15 minutes.[2] This is more frequent service than some large piles of overlapping routes in Sydney provide. It's also much easier to figure out and remember, so it's more useful, especially if you want to move about the city spontaneously.

San Francisco's network is simpler and more frequent precisely because *it relies on connections.* The purpose of Line 22-Fillmore is not just to serve trips that begin and end on that line. It's for taking you anywhere in the city from points on the line, via connections with other lines. It would not occur to San Francisco planners to add a separate "22A" that goes down Fillmore but then turns west to serve the Castro district, because while that would eliminate a connection for some people, it would add a great deal of complexity and would also dissipate the high frequency on which the whole network relies.

The trend in San Francisco, in fact, is exactly the opposite: fewer lines running more frequently. When forced to cut service in 2009, San Francisco's transit agency deleted entire lines that were too close to other lines or that overlapped other lines significantly. As a result, they were able to reduce service without reducing mobility to the same degree.

## THE FULL PRICE OF CONNECTION AVOIDANCE

San Francisco's local transit network, like many of the stronger inner-city networks in North America, aspires to a simplicity in which transit lines are like arterial streets. Your trip may require several lines, just as a drive or bike ride may use several major streets, but the high frequency on each line reflects an aspiration to make connecting as easy as possible. Obviously, connecting between transit lines will always be harder than turning from one arterial onto another. But the geometry tells us that the only alternative is complexity—a tangle of overlapping routes like Sydney's, where even high-demand trips are just too complex to figure out, and where the network as a whole is impossible to remember.

Here, then, is the geometry problem around connections:

- A Connective network covers the same area with far fewer routes. What really matters here is route distance: how many miles or kilometers of different routes do you have to run? If you try to avoid connections, you end up running many overlapping services to connect each possible origin to each possible destination.
- Operating cost rises with frequency and also rises with route distance. So if you have a lot of overlapping routes, you're running a longer route distance. That means your fixed operating budget will buy lower frequency or a shorter span or both, on each one.
- Low frequency and shorter span mean:
  ○ More waiting.
  ○ Greater likelihood that your trip, and thus your life, will be constrained by the transit schedule.
  ○ A higher risk that your trip will be disrupted by a reliability problem with a single vehicle. (High frequency, by contrast, means that even if your vehicle breaks down, another will be there soon.)
- In addition, a system of overlapping lines trying to provide direct service yields a more complex network, which means:
  ○ A more bewildering map and information system that can discourage people exploring the service for the first time.
  ○ Much more information to be learned in order to make each trip.
  ○ Greater difficulty in keeping the network geography in your head, which reduces the ease with which you can use the service spontaneously to move around the city, as people living no-car or low-car lifestyles need to do.

*To avoid connections, then, we must sacrifice frequency, span, and simplicity.* If we follow that back through our conceptual diagram from Chapter 2, we find we've compromised three of our seven demands for transit:

- *It takes me **when** I want to go.* Low frequency and short span make this less likely.

- *I can **trust** it.* At low frequency, a broken-down or late transit vehicle can leave you stranded. At high frequency, another will be along soon.
- *It gives me the **freedom** to change my plans.* Spontaneous travel is harder due to low frequency, short span, and barriers to understanding caused by complexity.

And yet, for all that, connections are still a challenge. They still deter ridership to some degree.[b] When I'm designing a network, I don't try to avoid connections, but I will use a range of tricks to minimize them. And if a transit agency decides that it prefers to be infrequent and complex so that it can avoid connections, I help them design the best possible network that reflects those choices.

So this is another plumber's question, a choice between competing values. We know you don't like connections, but that's not the question. The question is: Which of these two clouds of geometrically connected values are you going to embrace, given a decentralized city with many destinations of interest?

- Connection avoidance + poor frequency + short span + complexity + focus on few destinations, *or*
- Connections + high frequency + long span + simplicity + usefulness to many destinations.

As of this writing, the state government that manages Sydney's transit has chosen the former, though perhaps not consciously. San Francisco chose the latter, and continues to evolve in that direction. One simple measure of complexity is the number of separate routes and lines. In San Francisco, this number has been falling, as overlapping lines are deleted and planners focus on making the network simpler. In Sydney, meanwhile,

---

[b] The factor that modelers should use to estimate lost ridership due to the inconvenience of connections should be based on experience with existing networks where the connection is similar in speed and attractiveness to the one being modeled. Some modeling uses very general connection penalties, and if these are based on, say, typical connections in North American networks in the past decade, they may overestimate ridership loss if the planned connection is of higher quality.

the number has been growing, because new routes are added in response to new initiatives but nobody dares to redesign the historic structure.[c]

If you want to avoid connections, then embrace complexity and accept the problems it raises, including low frequency, short span, and barriers to new riders. If you want to escape complexity and build frequency and span, you need to encourage connections. You decide.

In the next chapter, I'm going to assume that you want to embrace connections, at least for some part of your network—not necessarily because you do, but because it raises some interesting challenges that we need to explore.

---

[c] Changing a network always requires political courage, even when the benefits are obvious, because people who are negatively affected complain at once, while those who are positively affected usually don't comment and they become visible only gradually through their ridership. When I redesigned Corvallis, Oregon's bus system in 1995, the local newspaper's coverage of the change focused on one senior housing complex, where people were enraged because I'd moved their bus stop *around the corner* to a different side of their building. Nobody in the local media cared about the dramatic improvements to mobility that the new network would provide. There are two morals to this story: (1) If your transit agency proposes a service change that looks to you like an improvement, send them a positive comment, because regardless of the proposal's benefits, they'll probably be bombarded by negative ones from people objecting to any kind of change. (2) We need better tools for making the benefits of a transit proposal visible to the ordinary citizen, so that a larger share of the population can make self-interested judgments that will weigh the advantages of a change, not just its inconvenience.

# 13

# FROM CONNECTIONS TO
# NETWORKS TO PLACES

If you decide to develop a network based on connections, the quality of your service will depend heavily on the quality of the connection experience at a few locations. Transit's ability to get you from point A to point B is no longer just about the service between A and B; it's also about a connection point C. In designing a connective network, then, we have to care about two aspects of each connection point:

- *Timing.* Is the connection point's position in the network conducive to fast connections?
- *Environment.* We care about three dimensions here:
  - Is it a safe and pleasant place to wait? Does the connection require a walk, and if so, is it safe and pleasant, both day and night and in all typical kinds of weather?
  - Does the site lend itself to reliable operations, keeping transit vehicles out of congestion or other causes of delay? (chapter 8)
  - Does it offer additional ridership potential? If a transit network organizes itself around connection point C, that means C will have an unusually high level of transit service, because lines will be radiating from it in several directions. So if the goal is ridership, the agency must also ask: Is C a place that will attract high ridership itself, so that we get the maximum ridership benefits from the high level of service that we're proposing to offer only there?

First, let's consider the critical timing issues. Then we'll consider the physical environment of the connection point itself.

## FINDING YOUR PULSE

The easiest connection you'll ever experience is probably a cross-platform connection in a major rail transit network. Trains on two different lines arrive on the opposite sides of the same platform at about the same time, then sit together briefly before they both leave. To connect, all you have to do is walk across the platform. While both trains are there, making the connection is as easy as moving from one chair to another in the same room. What's more, since the trains dwell while it happens, and both leave together, the delay due to the connection is zero. You proceed on your way at exactly the same time whether or not you change trains.

This may sound like a world-class connection experience that you can't replicate in your city, but in fact, even very small bus systems can get remarkably close.[a] In a smaller city or suburban area, especially in North America, you may notice a horde of buses gathered around a single platform or street corner. You may also notice that this happens every hour or half hour throughout the day. This event, called a *pulse*, is a way of providing fast connections even among services that aren't very frequent (figure 13-1).

For example, if our local bus network has several lines that we can afford to run only every 60 minutes, then the only way to provide reasonably fast connections is to coordinate all of the schedules so that buses from each route come together at a central point. At this point, the buses sit together for a few minutes so that people can connect between any two buses. Then, once that's done, the buses leave together along their respective routes.

Almost all North American small-city transit networks use some form of pulse scheduling. Many networks also attempt it in suburban areas

---

[a] Switzerland's intercity rail and bus network is largely built around pulses, a decision they made in the early 1980s for the purpose of improving the legibility and attractiveness of public transport (bus, rail, and other forms). Whole cities are connected to the rest of the country at the same time in each hour of the day—a practice called *clock headways*. These headways make it easy to remember the entire day's timetable at your stop. Once you are in the system, any required connections are usually pulses.

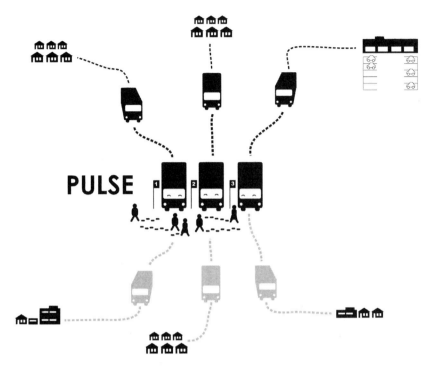

**Figure 13-1** Typical pulse of local buses. *Credit:* Alfred Twu

where local frequencies are poor, but it's harder there because traffic congestion causes more variation in how long it takes to cycle a route. That, in turn, increases the risk that a bus won't get back to the pulse point in time to make the connection, leaving people stranded.

Pulse networks can become quite sophisticated. Some coordinate multiple pulse points where buses meet (figure 13-2). This requires carefully planning the routes to be just the right length, so that the vehicle will be there at the right time at two different points on its route.

Of course, there's nothing about pulsing that's specific to buses. Trains, trams, and ferries can all be scheduled to pulse. Airlines often do something similar at their hubs. If you've ever noticed many planes from the same airline all lined up to take off at once, you were probably watching the end of a scheduled pulse.

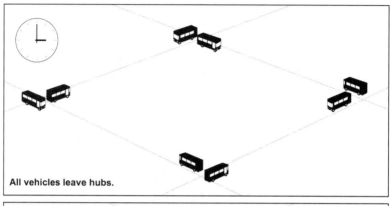

All vehicles leave hubs.

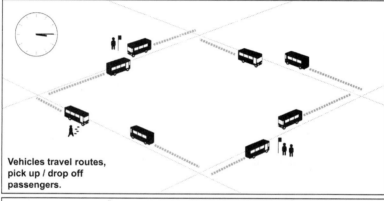

Vehicles travel routes, pick up / drop off passengers.

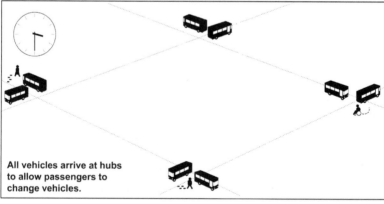

All vehicles arrive at hubs to allow passengers to change vehicles.

**Figure 13-2** Multiple-pulse network. *Credit:* Alfred Twu

## HIGH-FREQUENCY CONNECTIONS: FROM PULSES TO GRIDS

In chapter 12, in our abstract-city example showing the travel-time benefits of connections, we did not assume pulse scheduling. Instead, we figured your wait at the connection point based on the frequency of the line you would be connecting to. In our Connective scenario, all lines run every 10 minutes, so we figured that on average, you'd wait 5 minutes.

Could we have improved this performance further with pulse scheduling? If our services are running in mixed traffic, either as buses or streetcars, probably not. Even in uncongested traffic conditions, and with perfectly skilled operations, actual travel time in mixed traffic varies over a range of 5 minutes or so. For example, many major traffic signals take over 2 minutes to cycle, so if you miss just one you will lose close to 2 minutes from that one event. That's why most agencies that operate in mixed traffic (with either buses or streetcars) generally say that a service is on time if it's anywhere in a range of 5 to 7 minutes. For example, a policy may say that service is considered on time if it is between 1 minute early and 5 minutes late, a range of 6 minutes.

To do a pulse schedule with infrequent buses, you have to hold the buses at the connection point for long enough to ensure that any arriving bus can get there in time. If you define a 5- to 7-minute range of lateness as normal, that means all the buses must be scheduled to sit at the pulse point for 7 minutes to be sure that the connections are there for the latest arriving bus. The average delay resulting from a pulse would probably be around 5 minutes—about the same as the delay resulting from just running all the buses through, without pulsing, on a 10-minute frequency. So, when running in mixed-traffic (class C) conditions, pulsing on 10-minute frequencies doesn't make sense.

On the other hand, fully separated (class A) services have fewer causes of delay and can therefore keep to a more precise schedule. For this reason, they may find benefit in pulsing every 10 minutes, as many major subway systems do at key stations.

The better our frequency, the less crucial it is to pulse. If we can improve frequencies to the point where no pulses are needed, we're ready to discover one of the most beautiful geometric forms in the transit business: the grid.

## THE JOY OF GRIDS

Suppose you're designing an ideal transit system for a fairly dense city that has many activity centers rather than just one big downtown. In fact, let's assume for a moment that you don't want to give preferential treatment to any point in the city. Instead, you want people to be able to travel *from anywhere to anywhere else* by a reasonably direct path, at a high frequency.

Everybody would really like a frequent service from their home to everywhere they ever go, which is pretty much what a private car is. But money isn't infinite, so the system has to deliver its outcome efficiently, with the minimum possible cost per rider.

What is the most efficient pattern of lines that does the job? By "efficient," I mean the fewest possible route miles or route kilometers of service, so that we can afford the maximum possible frequency and that also allows people to travel from anywhere to anywhere.

We previewed this idea in chapter 5. Mathematically, the answer is a grid—a set of parallel lines, each far enough apart that everyone can walk to one of them, and another set of the same lines perpendicular to them.

In an ideal rectangular grid system, everyone is within walking distance of one north-south line and one east-west line. So, you can get from anywhere to anywhere with one connection while following a reasonably direct L-shaped path (figure 13-3). For this trip to be attractive, all of the

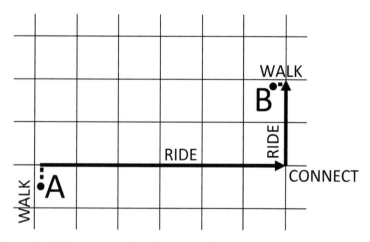

**Figure 13-3** High-frequency grid with an "anywhere to anywhere" trip. *Credit:* Erin Walsh

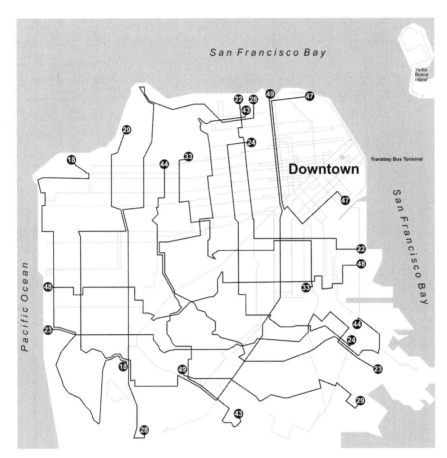

**Figure 13-4** Nonradial elements of San Francisco's all-day grid. *Credit:* Daniel Howard

services have to be very frequent, so that you don't have to wait long for the connection.

The spacing between parallel lines in our ideal grid is exactly twice our maximum walking distance. So if we're thinking in terms of ordinary local-stop bus lines, maximum walking distance is about one quarter mile (400 m), so our ideal spacing between parallel lines is one half mile (800 m). But in fact, successful grid systems run really frequently, so we can often afford walking distances a little larger than that, up to, say, 0.6 mile (1 km).

Grids are so powerful that dense cities that lack a grid network of streets often still try to create a grid network of transit. Look again at San Francisco (figure 13-4). The basic shape of the city is a square about 7 miles

(11 km) on a side, with downtown in the northeast corner. Because downtown is a huge transit destination, lines from all parts of the city converge on it, in a classic radial pattern. But under the surface, there's also a grid. To make this clear, figure 13-4 highlights just the frequent lines that *do not* go to the heart of downtown.

It's not a perfect grid, but it's even better. It is the grid ideal adapted to the particular shape of this city. Obviously, the grid is adjusted to follow the street network, but more importantly, the network balances two kinds of grid (figure 13-5):

- *Rectangular.* A grid pattern of parallel north-south and east-west lines, running continuously all the way across the dense area. Rectangular grids are ideal for large areas of continuous density with many scattered activity centers.
- *Spiderweb.* A grid consisting of lines radiating from the central business district and circular lines orbiting it. The radiating lines are called *radials*, while the circular lines are called *orbitals* or *crosstowns*. Spiderwebs make sense where you have a single, overwhelmingly dominant center of demand.

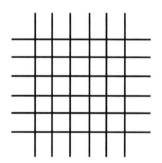

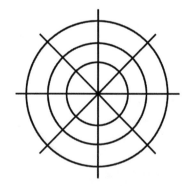

### Rectangular or Standard Grid

### Spiderweb or Polar Grid

**Figure 13-5** Basic grid types. *Credit:* Erin Walsh

Most real-world cities need hybrids of the two grid types. Often, you'll see a general grid pattern, but distorted so that lines bend a bit to converge on major destinations, sometimes forming miniature spiderwebs there. In San Francisco, some crosstown lines do a standard grid movement, flowing directly across the city in something close to a straight line, compromised, of course, by the street network (figure 13-6).

Meanwhile, the rest of the crosstowns take on various curved arc shapes, approximating the rings of a spiderweb that centers on downtown (figure 13-7). San Francisco's street network tends to push these into something like the letter L. Of course, plenty of straight-line travel is accomplished with these L-shaped lines. We used the north-south part of Line 22 in our trip from the Marina district to the Castro district, and it served us well as a straight line even though it bends later to complete an L shape.

Finally, let's notice that you don't have to have a grid street network to have a grid transit network. San Francisco has many areas with grid streets, but right in the geographic center of the city is a high north-south ridge where streets twist and turn to follow the topography. In figure 13-6, the straight-line grid elements, such as lines 23, 43, and 48, persist in trying to follow the same latitude or longitude even as they cross this difficult barrier. Line 48 has one more such struggle crossing Potrero Hill near the city's eastern edge.

If you study your favorite high-frequency, big-city transit system, you'll probably find that the structure is a hybrid between the rectangular and spiderweb grid types. Often the larger structure looks like a spiderweb, but if you focus on the densest area, you'll see lines functioning as a grid. A decentralized city like Los Angeles has strong rectangular grid elements to its network. In San Francisco's case, the relatively strong downtown requires a spiderweb, expressed in the many L-shaped crosstowns that resemble the lower left quadrant of a spiderweb's rings. But many of these lines are also useful as the straight-line elements of rectangular grids.

Finally, notice too that all of San Francisco's crosstown lines—whether I shaped or L shaped—try to get all the way across the grid before they end, so that almost all end-of-line points are on edges of the city. This is a common feature of good grid design because it maximizes the range of places you can get to in just one connection. If you look at the abstract grid

**Figure 13-6** Rectangular or "straight line" elements of San Francisco's all-day grid, excluding lines into downtown (northeast corner). *Credit:* Daniel Howard

diagram in figure 13.3, you can see how they would work less well if some lines in the grid ended without intersecting every one of the perpendicular lines. You would have fewer options for how to complete a trip with a single connection.

So, to sum up:

- Grids arise from the ambition to connect any two points in a city with good transit service, rather than selecting "preferred" destinations as radial and pulse networks must do.

**Figure 13-7**   Spiderweb elements of San Francisco's all-day grid. *Credit:* Daniel Howard

- Grids require high frequency because you can't time every connection in a grid pattern. If you don't have high frequency (generally every 15 minutes or better), it doesn't matter if your routes are in a grid pattern. It still isn't a grid network.
- To provide the most direct path between literally any two points, the optimal grid is usually the rectangular grid. However . . .
- Most cities do have some high-demand destinations where lines should converge to the extent possible, such as downtown. So, to the extent that your network needs to do that, it may logically evolve elements of

a spiderweb grid, as in San Francisco. On the other hand, it can also retain a rectangular grid shape but converge a bit around the major destinations, as in Los Angeles.

## THREE REASONS FOR A CONNECTION

No matter how smooth it is, connecting is still a nuisance, so planners try to require it only when the geometry of the network makes it unavoidable if we are also aiming for simplicity and frequency. Even then, we use various tricks to minimize the number of people affected.

To be fair, though, not all connections are justified in this way. Some are justified for political reasons, while others reflect the inflexibility of the transit technologies being used.

*Geometrically required connections* are the ones we've been discussing up to now, where the connection is required by a network that delivers frequency and simplicity for a many-to-many network. These are connections that can't be avoided in a network designed for maximum ridership in a high-density area. They include:

- Changing direction within a grid, such as the L-shaped trip that a rectangular grid requires.
- Connecting between lines in a network organized around pulses.
- Connecting between services of dramatically different speed, such as between rapid transit (such as a subway, monorail, commuter rail, or busway) and a local service, or between airplanes and trains.

*Politically required connections* usually occur at government boundaries, where you must connect from one agency's service to another even to continue the same general direction at the same general speed. When you hear people talk longingly of "seamlessness" and "integration," they're often talking about a political boundary problem. In North America, this may be the boundary of a transit agency, which may also be the boundary of a city, county, state, or province. In parts of Australia and New Zealand, you may also find politically required connections between adjacent private operators, each of which has a government contract to run service in that area, usually with government subsidy. These operators may be confined by boundaries among themselves that don't match any government boundary.

A whole book could be written on the problem that political boundaries present for transit agencies confined by them, and the various techniques that have been used to work around these problems. These problems are hard, but it's important to notice that when required to connect at a political boundary, you're having a political problem, not a geometric one. These connections are not part of a trade-off that buys you frequency and simplicity. In fact, if the political boundary wasn't there and the service continued across it, the network would be even simpler.[b]

*Technologically required connections* occur because you have to change from one kind of transit vehicle to another, even to continue in the same general direction at the same general speed. A connection between a subway and a local bus is a change of technology but is not required by the technology. Rather, it's required by the geometry of rapid versus local service. On the other hand, a change from a rail transit line to a busway that continues in the same general direction is required by only the technology change. For example, if you are traveling from Oakland to San Jose in the San Francisco Bay Area, you'll have to take BART rapid transit to Fremont, where it currently ends, and then change to an express bus to continue in the same direction at the same speed. The elimination of this technologically required connection, which interrupts what is otherwise a logical linear pattern of rapid transit, is one of the justifications for the proposed BART extension to San Jose.[c]

A technologically required connection is sometimes the ghost of a political one. When the Berlin Wall came down in 1989, authorities quickly reconnected the rail rapid transit network, restoring lines that had existed before the 1961 division of the city. Bus lines, too, were easily recombined. But during the years of division, West Berlin had ripped out its streetcars and replaced them with buses, while East Germany had kept its streetcars in place. Streetcar lines that once crossed the path of the wall, and which were severed when the wall was built, are still severed today because part of the line is still a streetcar and part is a bus. Today, you can still experience the Berlin Wall as an obstacle if you're traveling on local services. What was once a politically required connection remains as a technologically required one.

---

[b] The only limitation on this would be that reliability tends to fall as transit lines get too long.

[c] No opinion about this project should be inferred from my use of it as an example.

## FROM CONNECTIONS TO URBAN FORM

If you want to serve a complex and diverse city with many destinations and you value frequency and simplicity, the geometry of public transit will force you to require connections. That means that for any trip from point A to point B, the quality of the experience depends on the design of not just A and B but also of a third location, point C, where the required connection occurs.

At this connection point—point C—several things must happen that typically seem to be in conflict:

- Large volumes of time-sensitive transit service pass through, often including both rapid transit and local transit lines needing to connect with the rapid transit and with one another.
- Some transit services may terminate, which may require storage for vehicles and break facilities for drivers.
- A single location is provided with especially direct transit access to many other locations, due to the services converging there for the connection. This location may enjoy dramatically better transit mobility than anywhere else nearby, so it becomes a logical point to locate for people or institutions that value such mobility.

The third point is the biggest: connection points are the logical places to make big investments in transit-oriented development. If you want to enjoy the riches of your city without owning a car, and you explore your mobility options through a tool like the WalkScore.com or Mapnificent.net travel time map, you'll discover that you'll have the best mobility if you locate at a connection point.[1] If a business wants its employees to get to work on transit, or if a business wants to serve transit-riding customers, the best place to locate is a connection point where many services converge. All of these individual decisions can generate demand for especially dense development—some kind of downtown or town center—around connection points.

Such development is also welcome from a transit perspective, because the more residents, jobs, and activities are at the connection point, the more potential riders the agency has. What's more, if a rider chooses to live at a connection point instead of a local bus ride away from one, he or she will spend more time on rapid service and less time on local service. Not only is that good for the rider, but it's good for the transit agency. Remember: operations cost depends on cycle time, which depends on average speed, so rapid service is cheaper to operate than local service for the same unit of distance.

But when many transit services converge on one point, especially on the surface, they need considerable space for their stops and their driver break locations. These needs often conflict with the desire to build a dense, pedestrian-intensive center. One of the great challenges of urban design is managing these conflicting needs in the design of a connection point. Transit operations experts are often tempted to demand larger facilities than they really need, especially for terminating services that need to park while a driver takes a break. On the other hand, developers and architects often want to minimize the space allowed for these functions.

In the midst of these debates, it's common to hear someone ask: "Can't we divide this big transit center into two smaller ones? Can't we have the trains connect here and have the buses connect somewhere else, at a different station?" *The answer is almost always no.* At a connection point that is designed to serve a many-to-many city, people must be able to connect between any service and any other. That only happens if all the services come to the same place. You can sometimes move the driver break point to another location very close by, but if the services into a center don't all serve a common point, you probably don't have a complete connection.

This is a particularly tricky issue for connection points involving ferries. Since ferries can't come onto land, bus and rail services connecting with the ferry must come very close to the waterfront, which is almost always a place with conflicting development pressures and environmental limitations. Unless a ferry terminal is expected to serve only people in walking distance, it must have direct access by bus and rail transit. If there doesn't appear to be room for that, then the ferry terminal itself may be in the wrong place.

In my experience, the most successful centers integrate the various kinds of public transit into the development, looking for a win-win. This can be done only if it's thought about early in the process, because the transit needs may lead to a completely different design. I've personally worked on several redevelopment projects for suburban centers where a huge local bus interchange was perceived as a barrier to making the area attractive.

These facilities are often designed on the assumption that each bus line needs its own stop location, and that buses also need space for driver breaks separate from the stops themselves. These assumptions yield facilities that are so big that they cannot be integrated into an attractive mixed-use development except by putting them entirely (and expensively) underground.

One solution (not the only one) is some kind of new urban street that can serve the needs of the transit connection while also being part of an interesting urban center. In a plan for the new downtown of Surrey, British Columbia, for example, I worked with the consulting team led by Hotson Bakker Boniface Haden architects to develop an optimum urban design that was both an attractive and efficient town center and also a major bus-rail connection point.[2] Our proposal (figure 13-8) was a new civic plaza and street grid designed to turn the required connection into an urban design asset. To "animate" the plaza—that is, to give enough people reason to be there, especially at the early stages of development—we placed bus stops along two sides of it, with the existing rapid transit station on a third side, so that bus-rail connections would involve short walks across the plaza. Bus stops at the plaza were separated from driver break areas, which were placed on the ground floor of parking structures nearby. The design integrated transit connection movements into the pedestrian life of an interesting urban place.

While this concept was ambitious for a new outer-suburban center, many older cities contain vibrant public spaces where passengers making connections form part of the activity that keeps the place interesting. Examples include Berlin's Alexanderplatz, San Francisco's Justin Herman Plaza, and Athens's Syntagma Square. To find these opportunities, though, you need to move past the notion that connecting buses are a problem, like ugly utility infrastructure, and instead see the passengers they bring as opportunities to animate an interesting urban space.

One important tool for combining connections with civic space is the *inverted couplet*. In a country that drives on the right, we expect that when a north-south two-way street splits into a couplet—a pair of one-way streets—the northbound street is east of the southbound street.[d] That

---

[d] Readers in countries that drive on the left need only reverse every compass direction and "left" or "right" in this paragraph to get the same point in their terms.

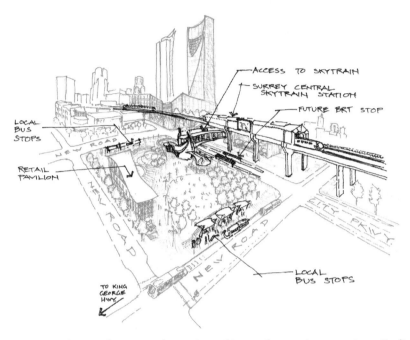

**Figure 13-8** Concept for a civic plaza animated in part by transit connections. *Credit:* Eric Orozco; based on a plan by Hotson Bakker Boniface Haden

way, opposite directions of traffic don't have to cross where the couplet begins and ends. That's great for cars, but transit benefits from the opposite. If transit doors are on the right and the northbound street is *west* of the southbound street, the doors of transit in the two directions open toward each other, so that it's easy to connect without crossing a street. In the Surrey sketch in figure 13-8, this tool is used to organize the buses so that they open onto opposite sides of a plaza. Portland's famous transit mall is also an inverted couplet.

To sum up, many great urban design ideas can follow from accepting the needs of connecting transit services into the structure of an urban center. With buses in particular, it's always tempting to move them out of sight, out by the rubbish bins, which of course sends a signal to their passengers about how unwelcome in the center they are. Good design pushes back against this impulse and instead finds ways to turn the abundance of transit, and the crucial role of transit connections, into a positive feature of the center's life.

# 14

# BE ON THE WAY!
# TRANSIT IMPLICATIONS
# OF LOCATION CHOICE

As we've explored the geometry of transit and the choices it presents, we've seen that the quality and cost-effectiveness of transit is determined by the layout of the community it serves. We've seen that the ease of walking to transit stops is a fact about the community and where you are in it, not a fact about the transit system. We've noticed that grids are an especially efficient shape for a transit network, so that's obviously an advantage for gridded cities, like Los Angeles and Chicago, that fit that form easily. We've also noticed that chokepoints—like mountain passes and water barriers of many cities—offer transit a potential advantage. We've seen how density, both residential and commercial, is a powerful driver of transit outcomes, but that the design of the local street network matters too. *High-quality and cost-effective transit implies certain geometric patterns*. To the extent that those patterns work with the design of your community, you can have transit that's both high-quality and cost-effective. To the extent that they don't, you can't.

You can still have one or the other: service that's high-quality *or* cost-effective. (By "high-quality," I mean "service that meets all of our seven demands and that serves all of our community.") Even if you live on the deepest cul-de-sac in the most labyrinthine suburb imaginable, a place that's practically designed to make transit difficult, you can still have high-quality transit, as long as you don't care whether it's cost-effective. Communities can and sometimes do run extensive local transit systems that achieve low ridership for the public cost, and they decide that this is worthwhile. (In chapter 10, we called these Coverage networks.) If you're spending only your local tax dollars, and your citizens want you to do that, then that's what you should do.

Your low-density, car-oriented suburb can also have very cost-effective transit that doesn't serve most residents. It might take the form of express bus or rail service that serves a station a few miles away. It doesn't come close to your community, but some of your residents will drive or cycle to it to make trips into the city. Of course, it may run only during peak hours when there's a strong market for this "Park-and-Ride" service; in short, it will be useful to a few people some of the time, but it won't be useful at all for most trips.

So once you've built a community in a form that's unfriendly to transit, or chosen to live in one, you will face a hard question: quality transit for everyone or cost-effective transit? Effectively, this is the same as the Coverage versus Ridership question from chapter 10, but a transit-unfriendly development pattern makes the question much more stark. There will be no getting around it. Decades of innovation have not found a way to serve transit-unfriendly suburbs with the same quality and cost-effectiveness that's easily achieved in transit-friendly ones. In fact, technology is certain not to solve the problem, because the problem is one of geometry.

## RECOGNIZING TRANSIT-FRIENDLY PLACES

So how can we recognize transit-friendly places, by which I mean places where transit can meets everyone's demands and also be cost-effective?

Often, this question is easy. If a frequent rapid transit line—rail, bus, or ferry—is already in place, the obvious answer is to focus on its stations.[a] Once you're there, the key remaining dimension of transit friend-

---

[a] Of course, a rapid transit station is ideal only to the extent that the rapid transit network is complete. A fragmentary rapid transit system, such as you'll find in many North American cities, will be less useful, except to the extent that it's integrated with other transit alternatives—and nontransit alternatives such as taxis and carsharing—that allow you to get to wherever you may be going.

liness is the quality of the pedestrian environment around the station.[b] Of course, a complete sustainable and livable neighborhood has many other important features, but the core of transit friendliness is in the proximity to the station itself, and the ease with which you can walk that distance. The effect of high-density development around stations is to give the benefits of the station, and its walkable environment, to as many people as possible.

But what if your city doesn't have a rapid transit system, or has one that doesn't satisfy your demands? Most big cities now have at least a few lines of something that can be called rapid transit, but most of these networks are fragmentary, with important pieces still in planning. You may also find that you simply can't afford to locate near your rapid transit system because the mobility benefits of rapid transit have pushed up land values there.

Every day, people who care about transit make decisions about where to locate things. If they can't locate near rapid transit, or if the city's rapid transit system simply isn't there yet, what should they do? And when developers and architects and local governments want to create less-car-dependent communities, where should they look to do it?

There are many facets to sustainable communities, but if transit is going to be one of those facets, we need a way to boil transit friendliness down to its essence. City planners, for example, need to be able to check any development proposal for its transit friendliness—not just in the easy cases, such as next to a rapid transit station, but in the more numerous hard cases, where we're somewhere in a currently car-dominated landscape and may have no idea what form of rapid transit may someday be possible there. This check needs to be simple. A city planner assessing a development proposal may spend only 2 percent of their time thinking about transit. The planner needs simple rules, rules that may not ensure perfection but that will at least prevent the common mistakes.

The same rules, if we could define them, would be useful for anyone who wants to locate anything. The average person deciding where to live, or locate a business or office, can't be expected to understand the details of transit. But the fact is: the transit mobility that you'll enjoy is almost

---

[b]  And, as we saw in chapter 13, the ability of local transit services to converge on the station and make connections there.

entirely a result of where you are. So if you're not a planning professional, the most important decision you make about transit is likely to be the decision about where to locate.

So, what are the rules? Here's a starting point. If we think carefully about transit's geometry, we can put most of what matters in just four words: "Be on the way!"

## A FEW ASSUMPTIONS

In proposing this principle, I am making a few assumptions about the future:

- *Urban civilization will continue.* I assume that while the next few decades will be full of surprises, they will not see the collapse of urban civilization. Anyone who has not embraced a survivalist lifestyle is making this assumption already.
- *Transit in the developed world will continue to be expensive to provide.* The cost of transit in wealthy countries is mostly the cost of operations, and except for driverless metros, these will continue to be dominated by the cost of labor. Regardless of the effectiveness of labor unions, we are unlikely to see dramatic cuts in the compensation of drivers and other operations staff.
- *Cost-effectiveness will still matter.* I assume that decisions about public transit will continue to be made in the context of some limit on what can be spent. Governments will always have to care about the cost-effectiveness of the transit investment, both onetime construction and eternal operations. Even if political shifts cause dramatic increases in what can be spent on transit, these increases will happen with the expectation of a proportional increase in outcomes, which implies that overall cost-effectiveness cannot be allowed to fall.
- *Ridership will still matter.* Cost-effectiveness, of course, can be calculated for any benefit (as we saw in chapter 10). If your goal is to provide lifeline Coverage service that replies to severity of need rather than to number of potential customers, you can measure your cost-effectiveness in terms of the options you've provided rather than how many people use them. However, urban civilization as a whole would

**Figure 14-1a**  Ideal geometry for transit. *Credit:* Alfred Twu

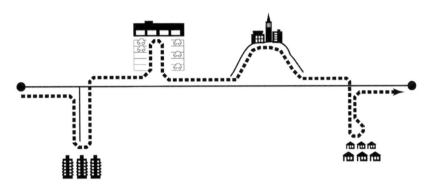

**Figure 14-1b**  Terrible geometry for transit. *Credit:* Alfred Twu

be impossible without extensive high-ridership services. Ridership goals will therefore still be a leading factor in measuring transit outcomes.

That's all we need to assume. The rest is pure geometry.

An efficient transit line—and, hence, one that will support good service—*connects multiple points* but is also reasonably straight so that *it's perceived as a direct route between any two points on the line* (figure 14-1a). Even if it's a U, O, or L shape, an efficient line is at least locally straight and thus able to be the most direct route between two points on a long portion of the line. (Again, this is not always a geometrically straight line; it may be a path defined by existing roads or rail corridors that everyone perceives as reasonably direct given the terrain and natural chokepoints.)

For that reason, good transit geography is *any geography in which high-demand transit destinations are on a direct and operable path between other high-demand transit destinations.* A bad geography for transit, then, is one that indulges in cul-de-sacs on a large scale. It sets destinations a little back from the line, so that transit must either bypass them or deviate to them, where deviating means delaying all the other passengers riding through this point (figure 14.1b).

When we hear the word *cul-de-sac*, our first image is usually of the residential kind: a short street with a big turnaround circle at the end, lined with nice homes. The attraction of this site is undeniable, in that it gives you access to the road network but has essentially no traffic at all. You can justify that in practical terms. You want your kids to be able to play in the street safely, for example.

The short suburban cul-de-sac street can be a problem if it obstructs the pedestrian and bicycle network, but good suburban design knows how to solve that problem: you just pierce the cul-de-sac with a segment of path, so that you have an obstructed network for cars but a completely penetrable grid of streets for bicycles and pedestrians (figure 14-2). This grid helps walkers and cyclists get where they're going without having to go out onto bigger arterial streets, even if the network forces cars to use those arterials.

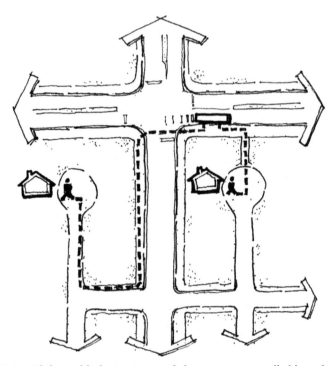

**Figure 14-2** A bike-ped link piercing a cul-de-sac creates a walkable pedestrian grid (right). Without it, the cul-de-sac requires long walks between homes and bus stops, discouraging ridership (left). *Credit:* Eric Orozco

Apart from that easily solved problem, though, transit has no quarrel with the short suburban cul-de-sac. As long as it doesn't obstruct pedestrians or cyclists, the residential cul-de-sac can work well in a transit-oriented community.

But consider these types of cul-de-sacs:

- A person who lives at the end of a mile-long dead-end road complains that the bus doesn't go by their house.
- A small shopping center or grocery store sets itself too far back from its street, even though the street is where the transit service is.
- A university, hospital, business park, or other campus-style development positions itself on a hill or promontory, often at the end of a road leading only to it, or on a road at the edge of the city where there is nothing farther beyond it.
- A new community or suburb is located in such a way that no cost-effective transit line will ever get to its town center.

Let's look more closely at each of these cases.

## The Long Residential Cul-de-Sac

In the early 1990s, when doing a transit plan for a small city in California's Sierra Nevada foothills, I had my first confrontation with the long residential cul-de-sac. I was riding a local bus along a major street when it suddenly made a sharp turn and went down a small, poorly paved local road. It seemed to be taking us out of the city, though I could see houses in the woods here and there. The ride got rougher as we went. Finally, the road ended next to a gate, beyond which I could see cattle grazing. The bus turned around, awkwardly backing into someone's gravel driveway. Then, it drove all the way back up to the main street and turned to continue in its original direction. I looked at the network map. Sure enough, that was the bus route. A bus made that deviation once an hour, all day, every day.

I asked the local transit manager why they were doing this, and the reply was "Oh, that's Judy! Judy lives down there. She kept calling and sending letters until we put the bus down to her house." You may think your transit agency is unresponsive, but some can be too responsive. Thanks to Judy's insistence, a bus was deviating to serve her front door every hour of every day, wasting the time of everyone else on the bus, even though she and her sixteen neighbors on the road couldn't possibly use all that service. Many small-city transit managers can tell you stories like this one. "Do you know if Judy still lives there?" I asked. They weren't sure.

Most larger transit agencies know how to say no to Judy. The problem with her request is not just that she lives at low density but also that she lives on a long cul-de-sac, so she will never be on the way to anywhere. That means that she and her neighbors must justify their bus service all by themselves, which a community of seventeen people is unlikely to do.

On my first visit to Singapore, a wealthy city-state where almost everyone lives in towers, I experienced a contrasting example. My hotel, the Elizabeth, turned out to be on the end of a cul-de-sac nearly one half mile (800 m) long (figure 14-3). Like much of Singapore, the cul-de-sac was packed with tall residential towers. But given the cul-de-sac, the only transit line that could serve these towers would be one that went all the way up the street, turned around, and came back. That means that the thousands of residents and jobs along the cul-de-sac would have to justify any transit service all by themselves, because they could not be on the way to anywhere else. So it's not surprising that there is no transit up the hill at all.

This problem would be easy to fix. From the end of the Mount Elizabeth cul-de-sac, I could see the end of another cul-de-sac coming from the opposite direction, leading down to another main street, Scotts Road, and the bus stop there. But there was a fence between the two cul-de-sacs. If you created a transit-activated gate in that fence, so that transit but not cars could go through, you would suddenly have a viable piece of transit line going over the hill. What would make it viable is that people on both sides of the hill could use it to get to *either* Scotts Road or Orchard Road, and even people who weren't going to points on the hill might perceive it as reasonably direct for their trips. In other words, *you'd be able to combine the hill's market with some other markets.* And as always, serving more people with the same vehicle means you can offer more frequency, better stops, and all the other elements of useful service.

## The Shopping Center Setback

Most urbanists know what to do about the suburban shopping center, and especially the "big box." These companies often prefer to locate behind

**Figure 14-3** Mount Elizabeth cul-de-sac in Singapore: photo (top) and map (bottom). *Credit:* Eric Orozco (map)

vast parking lots, often up to one quarter mile (400 m) from the nearest signalized intersection where you could access transit running in both directions. This location provides easy visibility to the motorist, including the ability to see quickly that parking is available. It also makes transit access unpleasant, if not impossible, and risks signaling to transit customers that their safety and convenience are simply unimportant to the retailer.

Fortunately, big boxes are built to last only a couple of decades, so as they wear out they can be redeveloped with the store close to the street and with the parking behind or to one side.

The larger regional shopping center is a bigger challenge. In some North American suburban areas, these have taken over many cultural functions, including festivals and exhibits that used to occur in public space. If you look at the all-day travel patterns of a suburban area, the big regional shopping center is a huge center of activity, creating travel demands in all directions.

If we want to provide even lifeline access for transit-dependent persons, let alone pursue ridership goals, big regional shopping centers must be connection points, with appropriate facilities to bring local transit service up to the shopping center building. As we saw in chapter 12, bringing local transit services together means being a connection point; geometrically, you can't have one without the other.

Some urban areas insist on this. In the Portland area, for example, most of the major regional shopping malls have direct local bus access from their surrounding area, and also longer-distance rapid bus or light rail service. The buses usually arrive directly adjacent to the mall building, often in a small "transit center" facility. In that region, you'd be unlikely to get approval to build a major shopping center without one.

## The Hilltop Institution

Shortly after World War II, everyone got the idea that the right place for a major institution, such as a college or university, was up on a hill, usually out on the edge of the city. The hilltop institution (figures 14-4a and 14-4b) is at the end of its own road, or sometimes with a network of roads that lead to it but never through it to anywhere else. These campuses will never be on the way, so the only transit we can offer them is what they justify all by themselves.

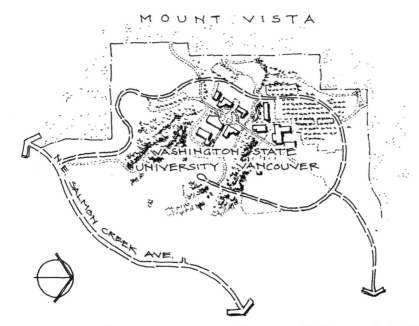

**Figure 14-4a** Washington State University, Vancouver, Washington. *Credit:* Eric Orozco

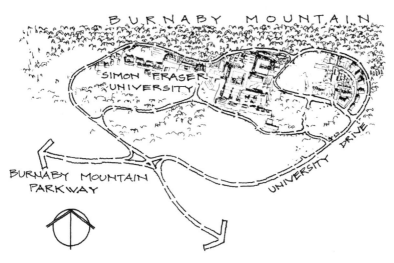

**Figure 14-4b** Simon Fraser University, Burnaby, British Columbia, Canada. *Credit:* Eric Orozco

Hilltops connect with deep human instincts. They offer long views, so hilltops have always been places to get back from daily life and see the bigger picture, as academia seeks to do. Second, altitude is often associated with cleaner, thinner, healthier air. We all carry the genes of medieval warriors who knew that the hilltop was a position of power, the place to build a fort or a castle. So when we put a university or hospital on a hilltop, we're claiming a bit of that power.

The medieval fort was also a cul-de-sac. It often had just one easily controlled gate, where comings and goings could be monitored. Because of the effort required to climb a hill, you usually don't do it unless the hilltop is your destination. So hilltops are intrinsically "not on the way." The roads that lead to the hilltop institution usually don't lead onward to anywhere else, or if they do, the path over the hilltop usually isn't the direct path.

Hospitals and educational institutions are both major sources of transit ridership, so these hilltop locations are a major problem if we want high-quality, cost-effective transit. The large university, in particular, is pretty close to ideal for high transit ridership: very high densities of people who are temporarily poor and therefore highly motivated not to own cars. To site these institutions on cul-de-sacs that will limit the quality of transit—and especially atop steep hills that also discourage cycling—is a remarkable expression of certainty that in all possible futures, everyone who matters will always have a car, and that cost-effective transit will never be needed.

Obviously, once it's built, we're stuck with it. Sometimes, we end up with fun solutions to the problem, like the aerial gondola that climbs to the Marquam Hill hospitals of Portland, or the similar one proposed to link a rapid transit station to the mountaintop fortress of Simon Fraser University, east of Vancouver, Canada.

But if a new university or hospital wants serious public transit, it won't choose a site that needs such a shuttle. Ideally, it will put itself in the thick of the city, where transit options abound, but if it has to choose a greenfield site, it will make sure it's located at a place where many lines of demand converge. It will want to be on the way.

## The New Suburb

New suburbs continue to be built on the edges of many of our cities. It's easy for urbanists to dismiss all of them as sprawl—a uniform, thinly spread evil. But these suburbs can take many forms, including some that have the potential to support good transit into the future. In fact, without changing the overall mix of densities, you can sometimes rearrange a proposed suburb to produce a much better transit outcome. All you do is make sure that the dense parts of the suburb are "on the way"—that is, located close to a place where a reasonably straight transit line connecting many other destinations can stop.

In other cases, however, the proposed site of a development may be so unworkable for transit that it's simply the wrong place for anything that aims to be transit friendly. In that case, the best transit outcome may be to build low-density, car-based development on such a site, so that the market for transit-friendly denser housing can be encouraged to locate in more transit-friendly places. That's the case with one of the most famous early efforts at "Transit-Oriented Development" (TOD).

Designed in the late 1980s by Peter Calthorpe, Laguna West, south of Sacramento, featured the now-familiar neo-traditional ideals for new suburbs. A gridded town center would consist of offices or housing over retail on pleasant, walkable streets, all surrounding a station for attractive rapid transit. Extending outward, densities would gradually fall, allowing for the large area of single-family homes that the market demanded while ensuring the greatest possible concentration of activity close to the transit stop (figure 14-5a).

In 2011, Laguna West is still unfinished. The single-family areas are all built, and they function as typical car-dependent suburbia, but the town center is dominated by large undeveloped blocks where the highest density was expected. Transit at the town center is limited to a bus once an hour, a feeder route to a light rail station 5 miles (8 km) away.

For years, we heard that Laguna West had failed because Sacramento Regional Transit never ran good service to it. Light rail has been reaching southward from Sacramento in recent years, but it has long been clear that there will never be a station at Laguna West. Even a frequent bus line to Laguna West is unlikely to make sense. Why? It's not on the way.

Laguna West is 12 miles (19 km) south of downtown Sacramento (see figure 14-5b). The west edge of the development is Interstate 5, while the east edge is the Southern Pacific line, one of the two major north-south freight rail corridors on the West Coast.

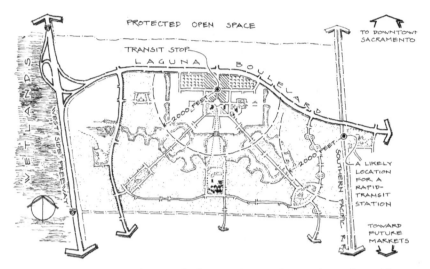

**Figure 14-5a**   Laguna West layout. *Credit:* Eric Orozco; from a design by Calthorpe Associates

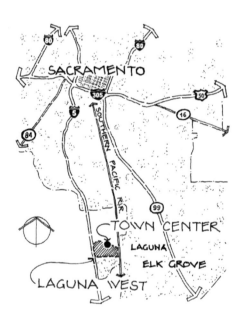

**Figure 14-5b**   Laguna West regional context. *Credit:* Eric Orozco

At the time Laguna West was planned, there was no transit to work with in this area. The bus system extended out to suburbs farther east, but there was no transit near Laguna West itself, because there was no development yet.

What should a developer and architect do when faced with a development parcel in this position in the urban structure? Locate town centers in a logical direct path with several other major destinations, ideally also where there's a right-of-way that could reasonably be used for transit in the future.

In this case, from a transit standpoint, the best site for the town center would have been on east edge, facing the rail line, which would have given it the best chance of attracting light rail. Why? Because it would be on the way between Sacramento and future suburbs even farther south.

Instead, the Laguna West plan placed the town center on the north side, facing an east-west street, Laguna Boulevard. Transit planners call this a crosstown or orbital street, which means it's perpendicular to the main paths of travel into and out of the city.

So, given this position in Sacramento's structure, what would a high-quality transit service to Laguna West have to do? Well, we could run an express route out Interstate 5, exit at Laguna Boulevard, and serve the town center. Maybe we could continue a little farther east to make connections to the local transit network, for people going to other places nearby. But downtown would be the main destination.

That means we would have a transit line about 15 miles (24 km) long that was useful for exactly one suburb, Laguna West, and maybe for another suburb or two farther east, but that would be it. There are no other markets with which this one could be combined, as you have to do to create a line that can support good service all day while being cost-effective to operate.

Laguna West is well sited for motorists, but when we start thinking in terms of possible transit lines, we discover that the Laguna West town center is a virtual cul-de-sac. Like the university at the end of a hilltop road, it can be served effectively only by transit lines devoted *only* to that purpose. It is geometrically impossible to combine its market with other markets, which is the key to building resilient, high-frequency, high-performing transit. So, it has the service that you can expect in this situation: not much.

I do not claim that the lack of good transit caused the failure of Laguna West's town center. Development outcomes have many complex causes. Nor do I intend any sweeping criticism of Calthorpe or the New Urbanist movement. Both have long since moved on and have seen great success in more recent years.

But Laguna West shows how easy it is to locate something in a way that makes quality cost-effective transit impossible, even while telling yourself that you're doing "transit-oriented" development. The mistake is made very early in the game, when you're looking at a blank slate and making the first decisions about form. At that stage (usually long before the first transit consultant is hired), developers and city planners need to be thinking about where the transit corridors will ultimately be, based on where the development sits in the larger structure of the city. This is one of the most important reasons for long-range network planning, integrated with thinking about new suburban growth, to which we'll return in chapter 16.

When planners and developers try to create "transit-oriented development" on suburban greenfields, they must negotiate with bankers, investors, and sometimes even governments who are still thinking in car-centered terms. A suburban development that isn't optimized for cars is a long-term bet on the success of transit, and long-term bets are hard to finance and sell. Laguna West's developer probably could not have gotten financing if he had put the town center on the east side, facing the rail line but at the farthest point from the freeway, because in the first decades, when the freeway would still be the lifeline of access, it would be hard to activate a town center there.

So the moral of Laguna West is not necessarily that they put the town center in the wrong place; it may be that the development site itself was wrong. You can design greenfield development that works for cars and also for transit, but Laguna West was the wrong place to do that, because its geography tells us that the car-optimal design would not be the transit-optimal design. Instead, when designing new suburbs where transit potential is important to you, you need to find a site, and a configuration of roads, that makes sense for cars now but will also make sense for transit in the future. Fortunately, we can find those opportunities, if we're looking for them. Here's an example.

## MOLONGLO: A CASE STUDY IN TRANSIT-FRIENDLY SUBURBAN STRUCTURE

During 2007–2008, while developing a strategic long-term transit plan for Australia's national capital, Canberra, I had the opportunity to work with the planners of Canberra's next greenfield growth area. Molonglo is to be a group of new suburbs with a planned population of around sixty thousand, located 6 to 10 miles (10 to 16 km) west of the city center. The area was protected forestry land until a January 2003 firestorm destroyed everything of value, opening the possibility of urban development there.

The decision to develop Molonglo was a trade-off between transit values and other sustainability measures. In the 1990s, the reigning authority of Canberra's planning was the "Y-Plan" (figure 14-6). It showed the city growing outward in only three directions, a "Y" shape, while the spaces between the branches of the Y remained undeveloped. Molonglo was one of those spaces.

The Y-Plan would have required ever-lengthening travel distances for daily life in Canberra, and those distances were already long. However, it would have been an easy job for transit. Strong radial transit corridors could simply have been extended, following the extending branches of the Y. This would have led to a city that could be covered by relatively few rapid transit lines, which means it would have been possible to raise the quality of this rapid transit—both infrastructure and frequency/span—to a higher level.

With the Canberra Spatial Plan of 2004, the Y-Plan was discarded in favor of a more compact form. Now, the spaces between the branches would be filled in, starting with Molonglo in the west. More growth would also be directed toward infill locations throughout the city. The result would be a city with much shorter average travel distances, which was a net plus for sustainability.

Sustainable urban form has many dimensions, and most of them benefit from overall travel distances being shorter. For example, Molonglo is so close-in that cycling—via scenic paths along the shores of Lake Burley-Griffin—will be attractive to many, which would not have been the case if this development had been as far out as the Y-Plan proposed. But it's a

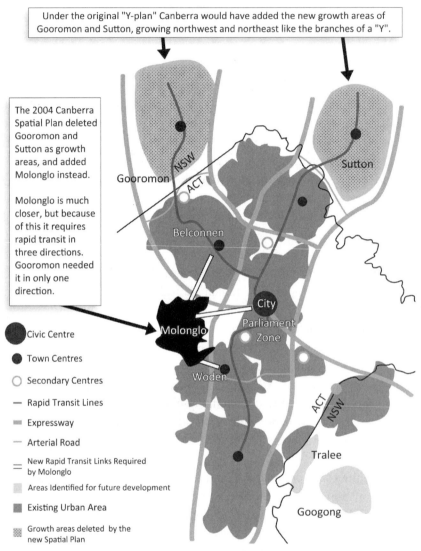

Under the original "Y-plan" Canberra would have added the new growth areas of Gooromon and Sutton, growing northwest and northeast like the branches of a "Y".

The 2004 Canberra Spatial Plan deleted Gooromon and Sutton as growth areas, and added Molonglo instead.

Molonglo is much closer, but because of this it requires rapid transit in three directions. Gooromon needed it in only one direction.

Gooromon

Sutton

Belconnen

City

Parliament
Zone

Molonglo

Woden

Tralee

Googong

- Civic Centre
- Town Centres
- Secondary Centres
- — Rapid Transit Lines
- ▬ Expressway
- — Arterial Road
- = New Rapid Transit Links Required by Molonglo
- Areas Identified for future development
- Existing Urban Area
- Growth areas deleted by the new Spatial Plan

**Figure 14-6** Canberra "Y-Plan" of 1967, and changes made by the Spatial Plan of 2004. *Credit:* Erin Walsh, from a base image from the Canberra Spatial Plan, Australian Capital Territory Planning and Land Authority, 2004

challenge for transit. If you imagine Molonglo's development placed far out in the northwest—as the Y-plan would have done—it would require a single rapid transit line, because when you're that far out, all of Canberra's major destinations are in one direction. But Molonglo, nestled in a space between existing development areas, requires rapid transit in three directions—north, east, and south—to link it to all of the existing parts of the city. That means it requires three times as many route miles of rapid transit as it would have required in the Y-plan position. And, that means a lower level of frequency and span on each.

At a more detailed level, however, the early involvement of a transit consultant allowed us to revise the internal structure of Molonglo so that transit would be as effective as it could be, given the location. In particular, it allowed us to press for a structure in which all the major areas of commercial and dense residential development—the areas where transit can expect the biggest market—are "on the way."

The first hard decision was to insist on only three rapid transit corridors instead of four. Unavoidably, Molonglo would need access north to the existing Belconnen town center, south to the existing Woden town center, and east toward the city center (figure 14-7).

But early work by a traffic consultant (figure 14-8) had suggested we build the main protected rapid transit corridor in a fourth corridor, south of the lake, directly linking Molonglo to the Parliamentary Zone, the main concentration of national government buildings and institutions.

There were two things wrong with this proposal, and they illustrate well the difference between truly transit-oriented planning and planning that thinks about transit as though it worked just like roads. First, it required service to branch as it approached Molonglo, and branching always dissipates frequency. Second, it introduced a fourth rapid transit corridor without effectively replacing any of the other three.

The branching issue first. Molonglo has a rough C shape defined by its main north-south arterial, John Gorton Drive. The proposed busway approached from the east, between the arms of the C. That meant that as it approached Molonglo, its travel demand would branch in several directions; some people would want to curve southward, others northward, others straight westward. The branching would happen mostly in undeveloped areas. So, by the time transit got to *any* developed part of Molonglo,

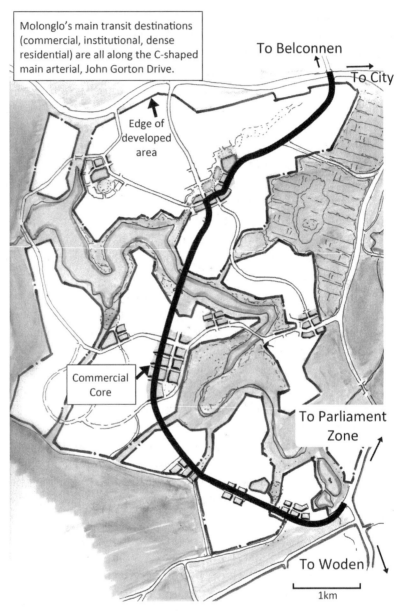

Molonglo's main transit destinations (commercial, institutional, dense residential) are all along the C-shaped main arterial, John Gorton Drive.

To Belconnen

To City

Edge of developed area

Commercial Core

To Parliament Zone

To Woden

1km

**Figure 14-7** 2008 sketch of Molonglo's proposed structure, showing placement of centers to work well with efficient and attractive transit. *Credit:* Erin Walsh; from a base image by Stuart Mackenzie, Australian Capital Territory Planning and Land Authority

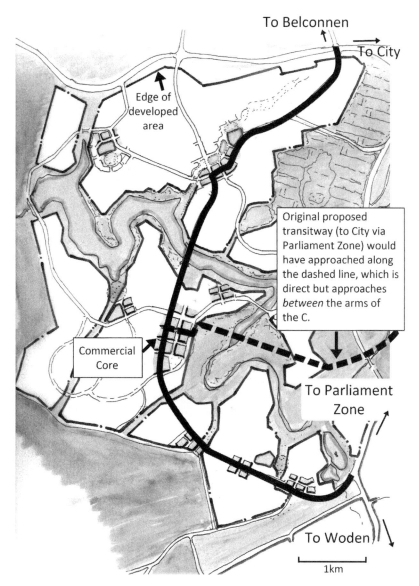

To Belconnen

To City

Edge of
developed
area

Original proposed
transitway (to City via
Parliament Zone) would
have approached along
the dashed line, which is
direct but approaches
*between* the arms of
the C.

Commercial
Core

To Parliament
Zone

To Woden

1km

**Figure 14-8** Original proposed transitway (dashed line). *Credit:* Erin Walsh; from a base image by Stuart Mackenzie, Australian Capital Territory Planning and Land Authority

including the town center, it would have lost much of its frequency due to this branching. That means that while all of Molonglo might have had fast service to the city, it would also have long waits for that service, and as we've seen, waiting time readily erases the benefits of speed or directness.

The fourth-corridor problem was worse. While it's appealing to have a direct service from a new suburb to the biggest centers of national government employment, the Parliamentary Zone, this is a heavily peaked market—huge during commute hours but minimal at other times. The main transit infrastructure of the city focuses, as it should, on all-day, seven-day activity centers, which include the city's commercial center, north of the lake. A busway would have been useful to peak commuters, and some services in it could have continued to the city center, but the busway approached Molonglo too far south to be the main link between Molonglo and the city center. The whole northern half of Molonglo would still insist on a direct link to the city center via the north side of the lake, so we would have ended up dividing our resources over four rapid transit corridors. Three corridors would be challenging enough.

Our counter-proposal (figure 14-9) was to focus all rapid transit in Molonglo on the single C-shaped arterial, John Gorton Drive, and to approach and depart Molonglo *only* via the ends of the branches of the C.[1]

If you're thinking like a motorist, this is silly. Why wouldn't we carry people to their destinations by the most direct possible route, which in many cases would be east-west? The answer: because transit travel time includes the waiting time imposed by frequency, and to maximize frequency, we need to run the fewest possible route miles of rapid transit service. The more distance we need our lines to cover, the less frequently we can afford to run them.

Approaching only via the ends of the C means that our transit lines can run along the spine of the C, serving many parts of Molonglo without having to branch. That means, in turn, that our frequency remains concentrated, instead of being dissipated as branching would require. In short, you may have to travel a slightly longer path than you would go if you were driving, but only with this pattern can we ensure that you'll have service coming whenever you need it.

Once the decision was made to focus rapid transit on the C-shaped spine, and thus to achieve high frequency there, the original urban design

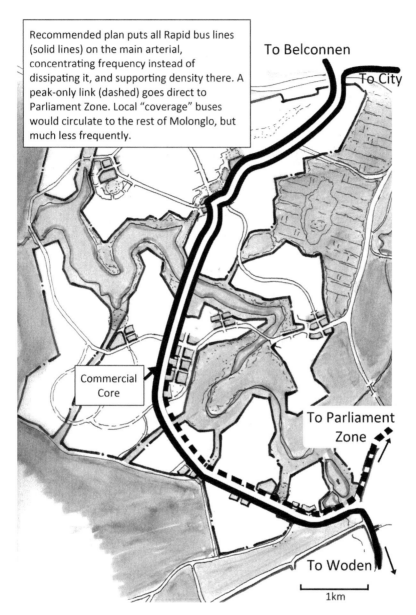

Recommended plan puts all Rapid bus lines (solid lines) on the main arterial, concentrating frequency instead of dissipating it, and supporting density there. A peak-only link (dashed) goes direct to Parliament Zone. Local "coverage" buses would circulate to the rest of Molonglo, but much less frequently.

To Belconnen

To City

Commercial Core

To Parliament Zone

To Woden

1km

**Figure 14-9** Urban and rapid transit structure for Molonglo as proposed by the author in 2008, and still used in 2011 as a basis of planning. *Credit:* Erin Walsh; from a base image by Stuart Mackenzie, Australian Capital Territory Planning and Land Authority

concept, with multiple village centers scattered throughout Molonglo, was revised so that the major village centers would all be on the spine. That way, anyone who chooses to live or work at high density will have direct rapid transit service, rather than having to rely on feeders to it.

Molonglo is mostly still in planning, with just a few suburbs under construction as of early 2011, and its development will take decades. Unforeseeable economic changes, as well as changes in fashion, may affect its final form. But Canberra's planning authority has still achieved something important. They now have a planned structure for Molonglo that takes transit seriously, understands transit's intrinsic geography, and works with it to yield solutions that make sense for the whole sustainable urbanism project. Molonglo will not be one of Canberra's top-performing transit markets, but it will yield more ridership, and support better service, because its planners thought about transit when they made the big decisions about urban structure. To the extent possible, they've ensured that all of the main transit destinations will "be on the way."

# 15

# ON THE BOULEVARD

A s we've seen, transit works best where there are many destinations
along something that feels like a straight line. One particularly
tricky thing transit needs to do is pass through major destinations (downtowns, campuses, medical centers, and other activity centers) in the middle
of the line without being slowed down so much that longer trips through
those points no longer find the service useful. We need to run fast through
those intermediate centers while still serving them.

Subways do this easily. Elevated lines do it with a little more difficulty,
because their structures, if not well designed, can be so unsightly as to reduce the attractiveness of the community around them. But if our rapid
transit is on the surface, we often face a conflict between the speed and reliability of rapid transit and the urban designer's impulse to slow everything
down to create a pedestrian-friendly environment. This is a persistent challenge in the design of light rail and surface bus systems.

For example, Portland's MAX light rail system is very effective in connecting various suburban centers to downtown as well as for circulation
within downtown. But the east-west crossing of downtown takes 23 minutes to go 2.8 miles (4.5 km) for an average speed of 7.3 mph (11.7 km/h).[1]
For that reason, the service is less attractive for connecting suburbs on opposite sides of the city. The system's intimate presence in the urban landscape of downtown comes, as always, at the cost of delay to people trying to
travel through.

**Figure 15-1** West Sahara Avenue in Las Vegas, a classic suburban boulevard.

This trade-off is unavoidable. If you want your rapid transit line to slow down as it goes through a rich urban landscape, you are making that landscape into a barrier to people trying to travel through that point.

But there's one setting where we've already built the necessary conditions to resolve this conflict: the straight, fast arterial street lined with commercial development (figure 15-1). Our cities contain a lot of these streets, and if we ever need to shift our mobility system quickly and urgently toward transit, these wide, fast streets, which I'll call *boulevards*, will be our salvation.

On these boulevards, speed has *not* been sacrificed to create attractive places; on the contrary, the road design lets a car fly right through at a constant speed as long as it has the signal. A transit service—bus or rail—can do the same thing, but with a stop at each big intersection. If it's considered important enough, transit can also influence the signal so that it doesn't have to stop anywhere other than its stations.

Car-oriented cities are full of wide, fast boulevards, usually six to eight lanes but sometimes even wider. Where they intersect, there is often commercial development on all four corners. Even in the car era, apartments have often been built close to these intersections. So while the pedestrian environment is often dreadful, the development pattern—a mixture of commercial and dense residential—is actually quite good for transit. What's needed, then, is a process of (a) creating the pedestrian links and crossings required to make walking to transit safe, and (b) ensuring that the transit service is fast and reliable, unimpeded by car traffic.

The goal would be not to turn suburban development into a lattice of pleasant town centers but, rather, to make it incrementally more humane, safe, and functional on its own terms, by gradually welcoming transit and the pedestrian. A huge amount of this boulevard-oriented development has already been built, so it needs to be included in any vision for a transit-friendly and sustainable city. It needs to be repaired in ways that preserve its basic functionality for cars for as long as that's needed, while recognizing the transit rider and pedestrian (and cyclist) as a person whose time and safety are valued.

Look, for example, at a very ordinary suburban intersection: the corner of Kings Canyon Road and Peach Avenue in Fresno, California (figure 15-2). There's a lot to work with here. There are already quite a few apartments, but they tend to open out onto the boulevard far from places where you can cross it safely. That could be fixed over time. With the existing development in mind, you'd identify permanent bus stop locations, each of which must have a safe street crossing opportunity. That could mean new pedestrian crossings, signalized as necessary, which could also be combined with other access needs.

Consider the southwest quadrant of the image. South of the east-west boulevard, there's a patch of apartments with several possible points of pedestrian access. Across the street to the north is a Walmart behind a huge parking lot. When Walmart redevelops, of course, you would want the building brought out to the street with parking behind it, but for now I'm thinking shorter term.

So I'd start by observing that if I signalize the Walmart entrance at the far west edge of the image, the same signal will serve a pedestrian access point to the apartments on the other side of the street. I'm about a quarter mile (400 m) west of the main intersection, so if there's a transit stop at that

**Figure 15-2** Opportunities to improve pedestrian and transit environment, Kings Canyon Road and Peach Avenue, Fresno, California.

intersection (as there must be, because it's a connection point), then I can put another transit stop right here. So, a signal here will have three uses: (a) controlling the car access to Walmart, for safer turns; (2) providing safe pedestrian access to the apartments; and (3) providing the safe pedestrian crossing that the bus stops require. When the vacant land just west of Walmart redevelops, we can require it to orient its pedestrian access to this signal.

These ideas are easy to replicate across the city. Fresno, like many US cities, has a grid of major boulevards spaced about a half mile (800 m) apart. That means that you could aim for local service with the widest possible spacing—one quarter mile (400 m)—which means you'd have stops at the major intersections and then one more stop midway in between them. Although quarter-mile stop spacing is ideal, we can slide this intermediate stop up to 300 feet (100 m) one way or the other to find the best site for a pedestrian crossing, based on the development and access points that are already there. We can then use this crossing as a focal point when redevelopment opportunities arise on the surrounding parcels. Over time, we'll build a more connected network for walking, cycling, and transit, without seriously obstructing road traffic.

So, to turn a typical suburban boulevard into a place where transit can really succeed, we would need to:

- Ensure that transit will not be impeded by car traffic congestion, through a range of tools, including full transit lanes where needed.
- Put transit stops at a wide but walkable spacing—perhaps a quarter-mile (400 m)—and make them permanent. As we saw in chapter 5, this is considerably wider than typical North American "local" stop spacing and in some cases may form a basis for combining rapid/limited and local services into a single product, for higher frequencies.
- Require a safe way to cross the boulevard at every bus stop, as a necessary condition for a stop, because you can't use a stop to make a round-trip on transit unless you can cross the street there.
- Look for a way to meet other pedestrian access needs with the same signals or crossing protections that the previous point requires.

I could also add more subjective values, such as:

- Ensure that sidewalks along the boulevard are adequate, including appropriate buffering if the boulevard is fast.

But we should pause before we go too far in this last direction. If we add too many design requirements that are derived from urbanist ideals, we can quickly lose focus on the reality of what the street is today and the level of improvement that's needed to achieve basic safety and functionality for transit, walking, and cycling. More critically, we risk spending so much money in one place that we can't scale our improvements to the vastness of the area that needs basic repair. So, when I look at a street intersection in typical suburban fabric like Fresno's, I see first of all a need to create a basic pedestrian-plus-transit infrastructure that will provide a safe and functional transit option for getting around the city, not necessarily an ideal New Urbanist village.

I've dwelled in detail on this ordinary intersection to emphasize a critical point that more idealistic urbanists can miss. Transit can work on these boulevards with moderate levels of intervention that are not hard to scale over a large area. In most cases, these interventions don't profoundly alter the nature of the current development and don't require increased density, so they don't need to be as controversial as redevelopment would be. These interventions can also be done either gradually or quickly, as the political moment requires. A program of such interventions would start, of course, with a policy adopted at the city level (with the support of relevant highway authorities) that lays out the kinds of moderate changes proposed, and the moderate levels of funding they would require.

## THE GREATEST CHALLENGE FOR BOULEVARD TRANSIT: CONGESTION

Politically, the hardest part would be providing transit with an exclusive lane or other appropriate protections from congestion. We explored the extreme example of San Francisco's Van Ness Avenue in chapter 8. The classic suburban boulevard is a little different; existing ridership won't make an easy case for a transit lane, as it does on Van Ness. So we need to argue more broadly, with more focus on longer-term outcomes.

The Los Angeles Metro Rapid has shown what transit can achieve on the wide, fast boulevard even without an exclusive lane. Now, on Wilshire Boulevard, the city and transit agency are making the case for a continuous bus lane, created at the expense of on-street parking during the peak period.[2] If this lane moves forward, as appears likely as of early 2011, it will provide a clear demonstration of what exclusive lanes can achieve. Then, the question will be this: If an exclusive transit lane can move more people per hour than a traffic lane, what justification can there be for *not* creating such lanes?

A few years ago I had a memorable ride on a Los Angeles Metro Rapid bus along Ventura Boulevard, from Warner Center to Sherman Oaks. Like Wilshire, Ventura is lined with density, including numerous buildings of ten or more stories as well as tightly packed midrise apartments and commercial centers. Like all of the current Rapids, the Ventura Boulevard service runs in mixed traffic but does enjoy signal priority. In normal traffic, Rapids often see green waves that deliver them from one stop to the next, a half mile (800 m) down the line, without stopping for a signal. But of course, all that falls apart when the street gets seriously congested.

My trip flowed smoothly through Tarzana and Encino, but then the bus got stuck in 2 miles (3 km) of gridlock leading up to Interstate 405, as it often does. The entire street was plugged with cars waiting to get on the freeway.

It made no sense. Cars can only fit onto the freeway at a certain rate. So in the current arrangement, the surplus waiting cars are stored blocking the entire width of Ventura Boulevard, choking not just car traffic but also transit and emergency services.

Why would a city give over the entire width of a major boulevard, and effectively shut down the street for both cars and transit, just for the purpose of storing waiting cars? Why wouldn't they set aside a through lane for transit (and perhaps also for taxis, high-occupancy vehicles, and certainly for emergency vehicles) so that efficient use of the street could continue even as the cars pile up? What would be the effect on traffic? Simple: the pile of stored cars would be narrower and longer. The increased length would have some impacts farther upstream. But meanwhile, people could get where they were going and emergency vehicles could get through to save lives and property. And if the transit lane moved more people per hour than general traffic lanes, it's hard to imagine a principle on which you could oppose it, other than generalized fear of change.

As our transit improves, and as transit passengers increasingly insist on their equal right to the scarce street space of our streets, we will see this question arise over and over. The fact is, we've already built most of our cities, and what we've usually built is a pattern where density and commercial activity tend to cluster along straight, fast boulevards. These just happen to have the perfect geometry for successful transit: everything is "on the way," and if we're protected from congestion, transit can flow rapidly and reliably between these clusters, serving a large share of the city's travel market far more reliably and efficiently than the private car can do. All we need is the necessary priority, so that congestion can't undermine transit.

## A BOULEVARD OF THE FUTURE

Let's stay in Los Angeles for a moment, because the urban transportation challenge is so vivid there. As I write this in 2011, Los Angeles is deeply frustrated about transportation. Once famous for the muscular romance of its freeways, it's now famous for random gridlock, 2-hour commutes, and road rage.

But something is new. Los Angeles has decided, mostly in the past decade, that transit is the answer. Strong majorities have voted to tax themselves for a massive rail-building program, and Mayor Antonio Villaraigosa has staked major political capital in an effort to accelerate it, delivering thirty years of rail projects in just ten years.[3]

If you know Los Angeles only from seeing it on television, you may still think of it as hopelessly car dependent, and in many ways it is. But the city's debate about transit is over, as far as the big money for rail transit is concerned. The debate that remains is about an even more limited resource: street space.[a]

Block-by-block fights about transit lane proposals can easily make us depressed about the chance for transformative change. But as the costs of driving rise, and as a generation raised with climate-change and peak-oil anxiety moves into positions of influence, more and more people are going to see that the boulevard plugged with stored traffic doesn't have to be the future. We will never move more cars down a boulevard—that's a fact of geometry. But we can move vastly more people, efficiently, sustainably, and reliably.

What might Los Angeles look like if this simple battle were won? And what might other New World cities look like if they won a similar battle? Let's use our imaginations and take a quick tour.

In 2030, the aggressive rapid transit program approved by voters in 2008 is mostly done. Rapid transit, mostly heavy rail and light rail, links all of the dense urban centers of the region. Dense communities are growing around these new stations, attracted by the spectacular personal mobility available there, and some new high-rise centers have developed. More than ever, greater Los Angeles is a constellation of many cities, with many sky-

---

[a] In the years following the 2008 global financial crisis, Los Angeles, like much of the United States, saw heavy service cuts, and the dire condition of the California state budget warns us to expect more cuts to public services. So, it might be fairer to say that the debate about major *construction* funding is over but a debate about adequate *operating* funds remains. But in many ways, the struggle over operating funds is also about street space. Faster and more reliable operations are cheaper to operate, so transit lanes—which would make the Rapids much faster and more reliable—would allow a fixed operating budget to run higher frequencies on more lines.

**Figure 15-3** A Los Angeles boulevard of the future? *Source:* Eric Orozco

lines, many downtowns, and many kinds of centers, all linked by rapid transit.

In all the dense parts of Los Angeles, people have the viable and appealing option of a sustainable-transport lifestyle, in which they don't own a car and instead rely on a mixture of transit, walking, cycling, carsharing, and the occasional taxi. Gas prices are high. Parking costs have been rising toward free-market levels as well, so even an electric car is expensive to drive and park.

The Los Angeles boulevard of 2030 (figure 15-3) feels more like a Parisian boulevard in many ways, including generous sidewalks, shade trees, and of course a transit lane. In the Metro Rapid of 2030, bus and streetcar technologies have converged into a long snakelike vehicle lined with many doors, so that people can flow on and off as easily as they do on a subway. Sophisticated signal systems ensure that nothing can get in its way, so it glides smoothly from one stop to the next past all the frustrations of other traffic. In fact, the Rapid is the only reliable way to travel down most of the great boulevards of Los Angeles, if you're going farther than you can cycle. And because it works, all kinds of people ride it.

The physical design of the Rapid of 2030 also helps it feel like an intrinsic part of the street. Guided by optical technology, the vehicle lines up exactly with the curb, at the same level and with a very small gap. When the wide doors open, wheelchairs and bicycles easily roll on and off, just as they would on a rail line. More importantly, the spacious Rapid vehicle feels like a continuation of the sidewalk, not really a vehicle at all. It's mostly transparent above waist height and features a slightly domed roof, so that when you're onboard, you can see the street around you and above you.

The Rapid, in short, has become a pedestrian accelerator, an easy way for pedestrians to move around Los Angeles *as pedestrians*. It carries them farther than they can walk while leaving them feeling, at every step, that they are *still on the street*—rather than on a vehicle that's using the street. They may have to stand, but they're not standing on a bus; they're just hanging out in an interesting street while moving faster than their feet can take them. The Rapid is progressing toward a new transit ideal: transportation that doesn't require withdrawing from the city into a constraining vehicle.

Because of that, the language has changed, too. Nobody talks about "Line 733" anymore. You might speak of the Venice Rapid, but really it's just an intrinsic part of Venice Boulevard. The boulevards of 2030 are "complete streets,"[4] welcoming and serving *everyone*, so of course they must have Rapids, just as they must have wide and attractive sidewalks.

After all, you wouldn't have a major boulevard without a Rapid in its own lane, because then there'd be no way for people to get through quickly and reliably without getting stuck in traffic. Your street would move fewer people overall, which would mean less economic activity in your city, which would mean fewer jobs. You'd be storing cars where they obstruct not just the transit system but also the economy, and people's happiness, and the life-saving work of emergency services. And that just wouldn't make sense.

# 16

# TAKE THE LONG VIEW

So, your city isn't ready to create transit lanes on major streets, and it doesn't have the money to build huge amounts of rail. What can your city or region do to encourage the growth of transit-friendly communities, so that great transit—service that is both high quality and cost-effective—can develop as an integral part of those communities?

As we've seen, the potential for transit in your city will be determined largely by the pattern of development. This doesn't mean that the whole city must be dense; average density is not the point. Rather, the pattern of density—residential, commercial, and institutional—must "be on the way." It must lie along reasonably straight paths that transit lines can serve, meeting at points where transit lines can viably and efficiently connect with one another. Those paths may be arterial streets, or they may be rail corridors or space you've reserved to build these in the future. They could even be a series of ferry wharves.

If you really want to coordinate transit and land use planning for your whole city, you need to do a long-range plan, looking about twenty years in the future.

As soon as I say these words in a public setting, I can see half the room shut down. Elected officials want to know what they can do in the next few years, and especially before the next election. Some in the room can't imagine caring about a year when they may not be alive. Overall, in our increasingly mobile culture, it's hard to care about your city twenty years into the future, unless you're one of a small minority who have made long-term investments there or you have a stable family presence that you believe will continue for generations.

But the big payoffs rest in strategic thinking, and that means looking forward over a span of time. I suggest twenty years as a time frame because almost everybody will relocate in that time, and most of the development now contemplated in your city will be complete. That means virtually every resident and business will have a chance to reconsider its location in light of the transit system planned for the future. It also means that it's easier to get citizens thinking about what they want the city to be like, rather than just fearing change that might happen to the street where they live now. I've found that once this process gets going, people enjoy thinking about their city twenty years ahead, even if they aren't sure they'll live there then.

The purpose of long-range transit planning is not just to create a list of projects to be built but, rather, to sketch the network structure of the future, showing how it will work as a network and how it will work with the expected shape of the city. I recommend that a good long-range plan concentrate on the Frequent Network—those services that will run every 15 minutes or better all day—because this is a level of mobility that can motivate people who care about transit to locate on this network instead of away from it. Any development that wants good transit should be on the Frequent Network, and any that doesn't, or that isn't dense enough to support it, should be away from it. That's why the long-range view of that network is so important. Your city will have other transit services twenty years from now—lower-frequency "coverage" services, peak express services, and maybe others that you can't envision now. But the Frequent Network is where you'll succeed or fail at creating new, transit-friendly communities.

So, a long-range plan must be specific about where the Frequent Network will be, so that land use and other infrastructure planning can be done with it in mind. Draw lines on the map as specifically as possible, to create a simple map that can be "on the wall" in the offices of anyone who makes decisions about development or infrastructure.

Steer away from technology debates. If your city is arguing about streetcars versus local buses, or light rail versus busways, draw the line on the map and commit to the type of service that will be offered (frequent or not, rapid or local). This can often be done without choosing a technology.

In fact, the best way to choose the right tool is to really understand the job you want the tool to do, before you even open the toolbox. So, for example, you can define a rapid transit line in an available right-of-way without deciding, yet, if it will be a busway or rail. You can also design a frequent local-stop service on a densely developed street without specifying whether it will be a bus or a streetcar. This is often a crucial step in getting buy-in on a long-range plan. Debates about technology choice can go on forever. If you put off your long-range planning until those debates are resolved, you'll miss many opportunities to guide the growth of your city toward good transit of any technology.

Now here's the catch: a good long-range transit plan (like a good long-range plan for roads and other transport) must be a two-way conversation with long-term land use planning. Now and then, you'll hear arguments that development should lead and transport should follow, but those are pointless chicken-egg debates. The process is a conversation, and in a productive conversation that leads to consensus, nobody cares who made the first move. Long-term land use planning (called "comprehensive planning" in the United States) typically goes first, because it deals with a more diverse range of issues, but if for some reason that isn't happening in your city, the transit plan can take the lead.

Another common misconception is that to have this conversation, all the relevant agencies must be merged, or at least forced to interact continuously as they do their work. In practice, this is a great way to make the bureaucracy grind to a halt; the coordination challenge becomes the main goal, and staff have little time leftover to do the actual planning work. The better solution, in my experience, is for the plan to pass back and forth between land use and transit agencies, in an iterative process, such as that sketched in figure 16-1.

The land use agency does a plan about urban structure. Then, transit planners do a long-range network plan whose core message is: "Here are the transit consequences of the proposed urban structure. Here is where we will need rapid transit, here is where we'll need frequent local transit, and here's where no frequent transit can be supported. Now that we've sketched this network, let's notice that here are some places where rapid transit will need to run but where you haven't planned any intensive land use yet. Consider doing that, land use planners, in your next iteration."

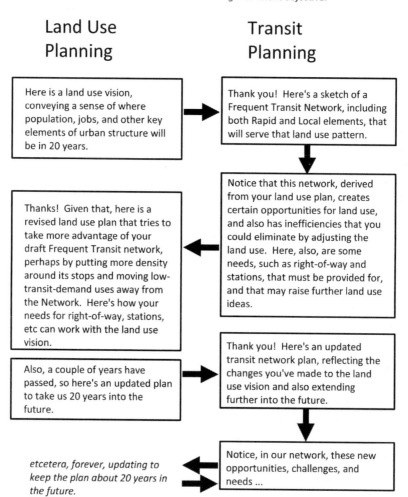

# A Healthy Long-Range Planning Conversation

*Similar conversations happen between land use and road planning, and between transit and road planning, and etc. for other other kinds of infrastructure or government objective.*

## Land Use Planning

## Transit Planning

Here is a land use vision, conveying a sense of where population, jobs, and other key elements of urban structure will be in 20 years.

Thank you! Here's a sketch of a Frequent Transit Network, including both Rapid and Local elements, that will serve that land use pattern.

Notice that this network, derived from your land use plan, creates certain opportunities for land use, and also has inefficiencies that you could eliminate by adjusting the land use. Here, also, are some needs, such as right-of-way and stations, that must be provided for, and that may raise further land use ideas.

Thanks! Given that, here is a revised land use plan that tries to take more advantage of your draft Frequent Transit network, perhaps by putting more density around its stops and moving low-transit-demand uses away from the Network. Here's how your needs for right-of-way, stations, etc can work with the land use vision.

Thank you! Here's an updated transit network plan, reflecting the changes you've made to the land use vision and also extending further into the future.

Also, a couple of years have passed, so here's an updated plan to take us 20 years into the future.

*etcetera, forever, updating to keep the plan about 20 years in the future.*

Notice, in our network, these new opportunities, challenges, and needs ...

**Figure 16-1** Ideal interaction of transit and land use planning on the long-term scale. *Source:* Erin Walsh

In a healthy process, this iteration continues indefinitely. Each round builds a tighter fit between land use and transit plans, and with other infrastructure plans. It also updates the plan to reflect recent actual events and extends the plan's horizon so that it stays about twenty years in the future. Of course, each round also generates short-term actions—actions that have been foreseen for years and are now ready to proceed. These become the work of short-term planning and implementation.

This conversation can be difficult in places where huge bureaucracies control this planning. The contrast is especially vivid in Australia, where power over urban transport and land use lies almost entirely with state governments. Enormous state departments of planning and transport, reporting to separate ministers, must collaborate to get their plans coordinated. It's like training elephants to dance ballet.

That may suggest that the best long-range planning is done by small governments, but of course this isn't always true. The trick is to decide which issues are truly issues for the whole urban region and to deal with them either through state/province government or a consolidated urban area government, such as Transport for London. Governments at that level should be doing long-range plans that show how major rapid transit corridors will connect the different parts of the region. These plans must be coordinated with land use planning at a similar scale, showing roughly how population and jobs are expected to be distributed among the parts of the urban area, and also where facilities that draw from large distances, such as seaports and airports, will fit in this structure.

City governments, meanwhile, must be doing their own long-range planning, consistent with whatever plans the urban region is doing. And here's an important point: it's often tempting to imagine that the whole process should be top-down. A city may tell itself: "Until our state/province or urban area government sets out a clear plan for the big picture of where the rapid transit will be, we face too much uncertainty to do our own planning."

Don't believe it. The conversation between levels of government needs to be like the conversation between land use and transit: a process of iteration. Higher-level governments do need some authority to override local objections when a critical shared value is at stake, but city governments also need to be able to get out ahead of their urban-area or state/province government. This is especially an issue for core cities—the oldest, densest, and usually largest city governments in an urban area. These core cities, the Densevilles of their region, have a more intense demand for public transit (registered in higher ridership on similar levels of service) than their suburbs do, for reasons that we explored in chapter 10. Increasingly, these cities are finding that the transit visions of their state or urban-area government are simply insufficient to support the intensity of urban life that the city wants.

Sometimes that means core city governments have to create their own funding sources to supplement what higher levels of government offer. And to do that, they have to have their own compelling long-range transit plan, consistent with their own values. Obviously, this plan needs to be consistent with what higher-level governments are doing within the city, but it may very well go beyond it, because it's in the very nature of these Densevilles to have more intense needs for transit, and lower interest in supporting car travel, than the surrounding Sparsevilles do.

Finally, the long-range planning process must dance with the short-range process. The credibility of long-range plans can be destroyed by careless short-range decisions. In 2008, for example, the Australian state of New South Wales, which governs greater Sydney, suddenly decided to build a rapid transit line in a place where the land use plans had never expected one. It might have been a good *idea*, but it was a disastrous *proposal*. By suddenly prioritizing this new line over other urgently needed lines that were in the land use plans already, the government contradicted the existing long-range plans. This in turn undermined the confidence of real estate investors, who depend on the stability of the planning system to assure them that building according to the long-range plan will be a good investment. Because of all these impacts, the proposed line aroused opposition even among planners, environmentalists, and transit advocates. After hundreds of millions of dollars were spent on planning and property acquisition, the project was finally canceled in 2010.

Sudden "bright ideas," such as building a transit line in an unexpected place, can be bad ideas for the region even if they are good ideas in the abstract, if their side effect is to make everyone uncertain about what, if anything, is going to get built in the future. Obviously things will change, but a good strategic plan identifies the levels of uncertainty where they exist, so that the degree of certainty, where it exists, is also visible.

On the other hand, short-term actions that proceed in the direction of the long-range plan can be a boost for confidence. Most successful public transport authorities, and the cities they serve, have a pretty clear picture of where they are likely to develop Frequent Network lines into the future. Often, they just need the courage to draw a map of that, and use it to start discussion.

So the conversation must go on in three dimensions:

- between land use and transport,
- between long-range and short-range, and
- between different levels of government.

In each case, consolidating bureaucracies is tempting but iteration is often the better path. The land planners do a long-range sketch of urban structure, and this goes up on the wall in the transit planner's office, so that it guides daily thinking as well as long-range planning. The transit planner does a similar sketch of a long-range transit network, and this goes up on the wall in the land use planner's office. That way, when developments are being approved, the short-term land use planner can check whether the location is a good or bad one for transit and can judge developments accordingly. Meanwhile, as the long-term land use planners stare at the transit map, they have new ideas for how to build communities around the proposed lines and stations.

These iterative processes scare some people, because they feel circular and therefore potentially endless. But every step is building elements of a durable consensus about a city's future shape, and at every step certain projects will move into implementation. The goal is to show everyone the transportation consequences of their decisions about where to locate, so that those decisions, expressing the self-interest of each player, collectively produce a more efficient transit system, and thus a more resilient city.

# Epilogue:
# Geometry, Choices, Freedom

In this book, I, as your consulting expert or "plumber," have asked you and your community four difficult questions that arise from the geometry of transit:

- Ridership or Coverage? Respond to demand or to individual need? (chapter 10)
- Connections (and frequency and simplicity) or direct service, which implies low frequency and complexity? (chapter 12)
- Peak-first or base-first? In any city that has peaks, you must decide if the peak is the primary product (peak-first thinking) or is a supplement to a consistent all-day product (base-first thinking). (chapter 6)
- Exclusive rights-of-way that ensure speed and reliability but cost more to build and take space from other users of the street? Or compromised rights-of-way, such as mixed traffic, which threaten speed and reliability but avoid these costs and side effects? (chapters 8 and 13)

I've asked other questions, too, but they mostly fall inside of these. For example, a choice about stop spacing will follow from the first choice. If your goal for a service is maximum Ridership rather than Coverage, your concern will be to run as fast as possible, because if people are optimizing their total travel time, it will be worthwhile for them to walk farther to a faster service. So a Ridership goal will mean a wider stop spacing. A focus on Coverage would imply closer stop spacing, to be sure you don't exclude anyone who may have limits on how far they can walk.

I've stated these big questions with an "or," as though there are two boxes on the table and you need to choose one, but only brevity forces me to. In fact, every one of these choices defines a spectrum. You can come down at any point between the two extremes, and very few transit systems are all the way at one extreme on any of these questions.

But it's still a hard choice, because to move in one direction you have to move away from the other. You don't have to choose a box, but you do have to choose a point on the spectrum, or one will be chosen for you.

The four questions are different, but there are interesting alignments between them. In each case, the first choice tends to be the better fit for cities that are highly reliant on transit, including London, parts of New York City, and many cities in continental Europe and East Asia.[1] These cities have a density, urban form, and infrastructure in which a free and empowered life just doesn't require a car. That reality tends to support the first choice on all four of the plumber's questions listed above. These transit-intensive cities

- have high ridership because Ridership goals, rather than Coverage goals, seem to be their intention. Indeed, without very high ridership, the cities wouldn't function.
- have connective systems, relying on people to get off of one bus or train and onto another. These systems are usually based on very high frequency. They have relatively high legibility as a result, and this legibility is critical to the sensation that you can move about the city freely without facing time-consuming learning curves for each trip.
- are focused on all-day travel, not just the peak. Their transit gets more crowded on the peak, and the trains and buses become more frequent, but the basic pattern of the transit network is there all day and well into the evening, seven days a week.
- have extensive segments of exclusive right-of-way, not just in their rail networks but usually also in on-street transit lanes for buses or rail or both.

Across the developed world, cities that want to be much denser or more transit oriented are leaning toward the first term in all four of these choices. They are valuing Ridership over Coverage, welcoming connections, thinking base-first rather than peak-first, and building or finding exclusive rights-of-way. This doesn't mean that transit authorities are always making those choices, but increasingly, municipal governments of large-core cities are leaning that way. These choices are following not just from the kind of city they are, but from the kind of city they *want* to be.

Not everybody wants that, though, and I'm not saying you should. If your ideal is a house on a quarter acre on a cul-de-sac in suburbia, with one car for every adult, then you should have that option. But you do need to notice that if you insist on high levels of service in your suburb, you may be presenting your transit system with a geometry problem. Low-density suburbs support some mixture of infrequent all-day Coverage service, which has low ridership and therefore high subsidies, or peak-only "commuter express" service, which has high ridership but carries the expense and inefficiency intrinsic to peak-only operation and is useful only for the commute. So, to live in a low-density suburb, you should expect to pay more (in fares or subsidy) for a lesser degree of transit mobility than an inner-city resident.

You can even live out in the country, if you want to, but to do that you must take responsibility for many things that urban people entrust to government, such as water, waste disposal, fire protection, and yes, personal transportation. Any transit service near your country house probably won't be very useful. It will also be very expensive, per passenger, for your government, so its permanence will be hard to count on. Understand those consequences, and then buy that cabin deep in the woods, if that's where you feel you belong.

Live where you want to live. Build whatever kind of community you want. Nobody is coercing you. But understand the costs, and don't expect transit to be both high quality and cost-effective if you live in a place where that's geometrically impossible.

When we think about our cities, we often long for them to be more supportive to us as humans. It's easy to shudder at the mass automation that cities entail and to feel that their sheer intensity is somehow hostile to our basic nature as animals.

This sense that automation and efficiency are somehow inhumane forms a strong undercurrent in many conversations about transit today. As soon as I talk about the structure and costs of transit, or why certain patterns are efficient, someone usually objects that I've lost track of the human dimension of cities. It's as though any mention of the intrinsic geometry of transportation makes me sound like a 1960s freeway builder, justifying how to bulldoze a city's heart. Such demonizing of geometry and efficiency is pointless. We must all live with the facts of geometry, and in a world of limited resources, efficiency denotes how much of a desired outcome we can create—even a humanistic or aesthetic outcome.

Sometimes, it may seem that we can avoid the hard choices about transit by focusing on the emotions aroused by a special vehicle: streetcars, monorails, cable cars, or whatever.[2] These vehicles create excitement and fun. The pleasure that arises directly from the technology will always be more vivid than calculations about frequency, speed, and operating cost, so these feelings of attachment are understandable. I feel them too.

But all transit technologies obey the same geometric laws. You can ignore these laws as you chase an exciting technology, but they will still be there in the end, determining the actual usefulness of your service. San Francisco's BART system, for example, can still feel modern and exciting, full of "zoom" and "whoosh," but none of that changes the fact that when a line branches into two, the frequency will drop in half, because a train can go one way or the other but not both. The same law applies to streetcars, buses, ferries, gondolas, and vehicles yet to be invented. Technology never changes geometry.

If we want people to embrace transit as a primary mode of travel, transit service must be useful. Usefulness, as we explored it in chapter 2, does include some subjective values, but it lies mostly in the design of the transit network and its fit with the geometric patterns of the city. If we cared about usefulness, transit technologies would be selected for their ability to fit those patterns well, and to serve them efficiently, so as to maximize the personal mobility of the entire community.

Buying a transit technology is like buying a car: you react partly to style and feel and partly to practicalities like capacity and fuel economy. If you decide you want to buy transit technologies based solely on style and feel, many books will help you do that. If you want transit to be useful, though, you need to watch the practicalities, which means understanding the geometry that has been the main subject of this book.

A great and humane urbanism, capable of conceiving cities that feel good and also function well, must rediscover these facts. The intrinsic geometry of transit must become part of the necessary geometry of sustainable cities, just as car-based suburbs reflect the intrinsic geometry of roads. Only if we embrace the facts of transit, and discover the opportunities they present, will our cities, and our transit, be human.

# Notes

## INTRODUCTION

1. In 2008, 67 percent of Los Angeles County voters approved Measure R. The measure increased sales taxes by 0.5 percent to pay for transportation improvements, most of it for new public transit lines, including major subway and light rail extensions. Two years later, Los Angeles resident Antonio Villaraigosa launched the "30/10" campaign, a bid for federal financing that would allow the thirty-year program of Measure R rail lines to be built in only a decade. Details on Measure R can be found at http://ballotpedia.org/wiki/index.php/Los_Angeles_County_Sales_Tax,_Measure_R,_2008 (accessed July 6, 2011). Details on Houston's rapid transit plans can be found at http://www.metrosolutions.org/go/site/1068 (accessed July 6, 2011).

## CHAPTER 1. WHAT TRANSIT IS AND DOES

1. These maps are at http://www.walkscore.com/transit-map.php (accessed February 11, 2011).
2. WordNet Search, "Mobile," http://wordnetweb.princeton.edu/perl/webwn?s=mobility (accessed July 6, 2011).
3. KonSULT, "Glossary," http://www.konsult.leeds.ac.uk/public/level1/sec17/index.htm (accessed July 6, 2011).
4. Saint Louis Great Streets Initiative, "Glossary," http://www.greatstreets-stl.org/component/option,com_glossary/Itemid,1542 (accessed July 6, 2011).
5. Todd Litman, "Measuring Transportation: Traffic, Mobility, and Accessibility," Victoria Transport Policy Institute, March 1, 2011, www.vtpi.org/measure

.pdf. Originally published in *ITE Journal* (Institute of Transportation Engineers) 73, no. 10 (October 2003): 28–32.

## CHAPTER 2.   WHAT MAKES TRANSIT USEFUL? SEVEN DEMANDS AND HOW TRANSIT SERVES THEM

1.   TCRP Report 95, ch. 10, "Bus Routing and Coverage: Traveler Response to the Transportation System," 10–34. The same figures are cited in *Transit Capacity and Quality of Service Manual*, 2nd ed.

## CHAPTER 3.   FIVE PATHS TO CONFUSION

1.   Cited in Commons debates, 2003-07-02, col 407, http://www.parliament.the -stationery-office.co.uk/pa/cm200203/cmhansrd/vo030702/debtext/30702 -10.htm (accessed February 1, 2011).

## CHAPTER 5.   TOUCHING THE CITY: STOPS AND STATIONS

1.   *Transit Capacity and Quality of Service Manual*, 2nd ed.
2.   There appears to be a wide consensus in the US studies that the most important break-point in the relationship between walking distance and ridership is somewhere between a quarter mile and a half mile (400 to 800 m) inclusive. *Transit Capacity and Quality of Service Manual*, 2nd ed., for example, observes that about 80 percent of transit riders walk less than this distance (pp. 3–10) and implicitly endorses this standard. Transit riders walk various distances, but this seems to be an inflection point beyond which very few customers can be expected to walk. See also G. B. Arrington and Robert Cervero, *Effects of TOD on Housing, Parking, and Travel*, TCRP Report 128 (Washington, DC: Transportation Research Board, 2008); Robert Cervero, Christopher Ferrell, and Steven Murphy *Transit-Oriented Development and Joint Development in the United States: A Literature Review*, Research Results Digest no. 52 (Washington, DC: Transit Cooperative Research Program, 2002).
3.   From Urban Design 4 Health, via Harvard Business Review, "The Unintended Consequences of Cul-de-Sacs," http://hbr.org/2010/05/back-to-the-city/sb1 (accessed June 30, 2011).

4. *Transit Capacity and Quality of Service Manual*, 2nd ed., notes that acceptable walking distances decline at grades above 5 percent (pp. 3–10).

5. HiTrans, *Public Transport: Planning the Networks* (Stavanger, Norway: HiTrans, 2005), v.2, 127. Though focused on cities under 500,000, the HiTrans guides provide an excellent view of European transit practice and theory. See http://www.hitrans.org (accessed June 30, 2011).

6. Many European cities have local-stop streetcar/trams, many dating from before the advent of the car. In North America and Australasia, the only cities to retain substantial networks of these were Melbourne, New Orleans, and Toronto, though some cities retain one or two historic lines and fragments are now operated as part of light rail networks in San Francisco, Boston, and some other cities. Modern streetcars in the New World include those in Portland and Seattle, with many others under development.

7. Vukan Vuchic insists that "rapid" also must imply a totally exclusive and grade-separated right-of-way, a different distinction that we'll explore in chapter 8. Vukan Vuchic, *Urban Transit: Operations, Planning, and Economics* (Hoboken NJ: John Wiley, 2005), app. 3, p. 628.

8. Los Angeles County Metropolitan Transportation Authority, "Wilshire Bus Rapid Transit Project," http://www.metro.net/projects/wilshire (accessed July 6, 2011).

9. Information provided by the Los Angeles County Metropolitan Transportation Authority. The common productivity measure of boardings/hour values all riders equally, regardless of how far they are going. If you use it to compare one line to another, lines that are geared for shorter trips will tend to look better, because they turn over passengers frequently and therefore generate a high number of boardings without reaching capacity limits. Given the length of the trips it serves, the Wilshire Rapid's performance of more than 60 boardings/hour is exceptional.

10. For example, in the 1990s, Seattle's King County Metro consolidated local service and two limited-stop services on long and busy Aurora Avenue. The resulting service, now called Line 358, has wider stop spacing than the former local but more stops than former limited-stop lines. The decision was influenced by a service planning study that demonstrated that 75 percent of the line's daily ridership occurred at less than a third of the stops.

## CHAPTER 6.  PEAK OR ALL DAY?

1. Kitsap Transit, "Worker/Driver Program," http://www.kitsaptransit.org /WorkerDriverBusProgram.html (accessed July 6, 2011).

## CHAPTER 7.   FREQUENCY IS FREEDOM

1.  King County Metro Transit, "Map: Metro System," http://metro.kingcounty
    .gov/tops/bus/psystem_map.html (accessed July 6, 2011).
2.  Metro Transit, "Hi-Frequency Service Network" (map), http://www.metro
    transit.org/high-frequency-network-map.aspx (accessed June 30, 2011).
3.  Metro Transit, "Regional System and Downtown Maps," http://www.metro
    transit.org/maps-schedules.aspx; click on "Regional System and Downtown
    Maps" tab (accessed June 30, 2011).
4.  A collection of these spanning most of the United States' major river systems
    is available at http://somethingaboutmaps.wordpress.com/river-maps (ac-
    cessed June 30, 2011).

## CHAPTER 8.   THE OBSTACLE COURSE:
## SPEED, DELAY, AND RELIABILITY

1.  Tracy Chapman, "Fast Car," *Tracy Chapman* (Electra/Asylum Records, 1988).
2.  Vuchic, *Urban Transit*, 553–58.
3.  All figures in this section are from San Francisco County Transportation
    Authority, *Van Ness BRT Study* (2–26), http://www.sfcta.org/images/stories
    /Planning/VanNessAvenueBusRapidTransit/section2_2006me.pdf (accessed
    February 4, 2011).
4.  As of March 2011, the Portland Streetcar was scheduled to take 22 minutes
    to cover the 2.32 miles from NW 23rd & Marshall to SW 5th & Mont-
    gomery, an average speed of 6.3 miles per hour. Portland Streetcar schedule
    brochure, http://www.portlandstreetcar.org/node/3 (accessed March 13,
    2011).
5.  From Graham Currie, "Planning and Design for On Road Public Transport,"
    in *Traffic Engineering and Management* (Institute of Transport Studies, Monash
    University, ISBM no. 0 7326 1612 3).

## CHAPTER 9.   DENSITY DISTRACTIONS

1.  Jed Kolko, for example, finds that across the United States, employment den-
    sity affects ridership more strongly than residential density does. Jeff Kolko,
    "Density, Employment Growth, and Ridership around New Stations" (Public
    Policy Institute of California, 2011). This is understandable when you con-
    sider that most US cities have long had areas of very high employment den-

sity ("downtown") and that transit systems have historically been oriented toward those centers. The relationship between residential density and ridership is also clear but its shape is more subtle and its political impact more profound.

2. Paul Mees, *Transport for Suburbia: Beyond the Automobile Age* (London: Earthscan, 2010), 7.

3. Mees, *Transport for Suburbia*, fig 4.1, p. 60. For another implicit critique of Mees's method that reaches my conclusions with greater statistical rigor, see Eric Eidlin, "What Density Doesn't Tell Us about Sprawl," *Access 37* (2010), University of California Transportation Center (http://www.uctc.net), pp. 1–9; available at http://www.uctc.net/access/37/access37_sprawl.shtml (accessed July 6, 2011).

4. Peter Newman and Jeffrey Kenworthy, *Sustainability and Cities: Overcoming Automobile Dependence* (Washington, DC: Island Press, 1999).

## CHAPTER 10. RIDERSHIP OR COVERAGE?
## THE CHALLENGE OF SERVICE ALLOCATION

1. See, for example, persistent anti-transit arguments that require comparing transit's environmental benefit with its total costs and emissions, even though some of those costs and emissions are the result of pursuing Coverage goals where environmental benefit is not the objective. For example, Kevin Libin in Canada's *National Post*: "On quieter routes, the average city bus usually undoes whatever efficiencies are gained during the few hours a day, on the few routes, where transit is at its peak." Kevin Libin, "Rethinking Green: Save the Environment: Don't Take transit" *National Post*, December 7, 2009, http://www.nationalpost.com/news/story.html?id=2314104 (accessed June 30, 2011). The "quieter routes," of course, are the Coverage network, where high ridership is not the objective..

2. Parsons Brinckerhoff Quade and Douglas, *Transit and Urban Form*, TCRP Report 16 (Washington, DC: National Academy Press and U.S. Transit Development Corporation and Research Council, 1996).

3. R. J. Spillar and G. S. Rutherford, "The Effects of Population Density and Income on Per Capita Transit Ridership in Western American Cities," *Institute of Transportation Engineers' Compendium of Technical Papers*, 60th Annual Meeting, August 5–8, 1998 (pp. 327–31). Similar research that I led in 1994 for Portland's transit agency Tri-Met found a strong correlation between ridership and the square of the density (both residential and commercial). See Nelson/Nygaard Consulting Associates, "Land use and Transit Demand:

The Transit Orientation Index," ch. 3 in *Primary Transit Network Study* (draft) (Portland, OR: Tri-Met, 1995). Back in 1977, Pushkarev and Zupan's study of large urban areas also articulated the same results for the lower part of the density range, observing that transit demand varied minimally below seven dwelling units/acre but rose in a more pronounced way in response to density beyond that level. Boris S. Pushkarev and Jeffrey M. Zupan, *Public Transportation and Land Use Policy: A Regional Plan Association Book* (Bloomington: Indiana University Press, 1977), 30.

4.  Rail rapid transit, in particular, has typically depended heavily on the single intense downtown, especially in the United States, Canada, and Australia. Pushkarev and Zupan, *Public Transportation and Land Use Policy* (p. 28), found a strong correlation between rail transit ridership and the square feet of floor space in the region's largest central business district, the latter used as a reasonable proxy for downtown intensity, based on 1974 data. These calculations have since grown more complex with the rise of secondary high-rise employment and activity centers in many urban regions, but a strong link between the size of high-rise employment centers and transit ridership continues to be observed. See also Kolko, "Density, Employment Growth, and Ridership."

5.  The Reno area policy, developed with the assistance of the author, states: "Approximately 80% of RTC RIDE service will be allocated to maximize productivity and 20% for coverage to provide service in less dense areas." Regional Transportation Authority of Washoe County Nevada *Washoe County 2030 Regional Transportation Plan* (2005), ch. 2, pp. 2–7, http://www.rtcwashoe.com/planning-7 (accessed June 30, 2011).

6.  See note 1 earlier in this chapter.

## CHAPTER 11. CAN FARES BE FAIR?

1.  For example, Randal O'Toole writes: "Unlike transit, [US] interstate highways were funded out of user feeds, creating a feedback loop: if planners built more interstates that people wanted to use, users would pay the taxes needed to fund the roads." Randal O'Toole, *Fixing Transit: The Case for Privatization*, Policy Analysis 670, Cato Institute, www.cato.org/pubs/pas /PA670.pdf (accessed June 30, 2011).

2.  Donald Shoup, *The High Cost of Free Parking* (Chicago: Planners Press, 2005).

3.  See Martin Wachs, "Improving Efficiency and Equity in Transportation Finance," Brookings Institution (2003), http://www.brookings.edu/reports

/2003/04transportation_wachs.aspx (accessed July 6, 2011). See also U.S. PIRG, "Do Roads Pay for Themselves? Setting the Record Straight on Transportation Finance" (January 4, 2011), http://www.uspirg.org/home /reports/report-archives/transportation/transportation2/do-roads-pay-for -themselves-setting-the-record-straight-on-transportation-funding (accessed July 6, 2011).

4. The website Free Public Transit Success, http://fptsuccess.blogspot.com/ (accessed July 6, 2011), maintains a list of fare-free agencies, though many are fare-free only at certain times of day or on certain services. Logan, Utah's Cache Valley Transit District explains its fare-free policy here: http://www .cvtdbus.org/news/farefreepolicy.php (accessed July 6, 2011). Island Transit on Whidbey and Camano Islands, Washington explains, its fare-free policy here: http://islandtransit.org/did_You_Know/ (accessed July 6, 2011).

5. See "Independent Public Inquiry: Sydney's Long Term Public Transport Plan," ch. 4 (May 2010), http://transportpublicinquiry.com.au/ (accessed July 6, 2011).

6. "Metro Fares," http://metro.kingcounty.gov/tops/bus/fare/fare-info.html (accessed February 11, 2011).

7. Although the fare is free, it still requires a free ticket, a level of hassle designed to exclude spontaneous use. See http://www.metlinkmelbourne.com .au/fares-tickets/metropolitan-fares-and-tickets/metcard/metcard-types/#17 (accessed February 11, 2011).

## CHAPTER 12. CONNECTIONS OR COMPLEXITY?

1. All references to routes and schedules in this chapter are as of November 28, 2010.

2. 511.org, "Agency Schedule and Route Selector," http://transit.511.org /schedules/index.aspx?#m1=S&m2=bus&routeid=25294&cid=SF (accessed November 28, 2010).

## CHAPTER 13. FROM CONNECTIONS TO NETWORKS TO PLACES

1. Mapnificent is at http://www.mapnificent.net (accessed July 6, 2011). Walk Score, "Transit Time Map: Bay Area, 9:00am," http://www.walkscore.com /transit-map.php (accessed July 6, 2011).

2. Now part of DIALOG, http://www.designdialog.ca/ (accessed June 30, 2011).

## CHAPTER 14.  BE ON THE WAY! TRANSIT IMPLICATIONS OF LOCATION CHOICE

1.  McCormick Rankin Cagney, ACT Strategic Public Transport Network Plan, Final Report, 2009. http://www.tams.act.gov.au/move/sustainable_transport /sustainable_transport_action_plan/public_transport (accessed June 30, 2011). Discussion of Molonglo is in chapter 8.

## CHAPTER 15.  ON THE BOULEVARD

1.  Travel time from Lloyd Center to Goose Hollow at 1:00 p.m. on a weekday, per TriMet Trip Planner in February 2011, http://trimet.org/index.htm.
2.  Los Angeles Country Metropolitan Transportation Authority, "Wilshire Bus Rapid Transit Project," http://www.metro.net/projects/wilshire/ (accessed March 15, 2011).
3.  The acceleration plan, originally called "30/10," urges Congress to develop a new federal lending capability that could lend against the 30 years of approved sales tax funds to build the intended projects in 10 years. The concept generated significant support from other cities that might benefit from a similar arrangement. In February 2011 the campaign was rechristened America Fast Forward, reflecting this nationwide interest. See http://americafastforward.org/ (accessed June 30, 2011).
4.  For information on the related Complete Streets movement, see http://www .completestreets.org (accessed June 30, 2011).

## EPILOGUE: GEOMETRY, CHOICES, FREEDOM

1.  I am referring here, as throughout the book, to "developed" or relatively wealthy countries, so "East Asia" in this sense primarily means Japan, South Korea, Hong Kong, and Singapore, though of course other countries are moving into this club.
2.  For a book-length exploration of how much fun these vehicles can be, see Darrin Nordahl, My Kind of Transit: Rethinking Public Transportation in America (Chicago: Center for American Places, 2008). The book can be criticized for being unaware of the costs and real-world trade-offs presented by these "fun" vehicles, and for implying (falsely, in my experience) that transit professionals are unaware of how "fun" can contribute to transit outcomes. Still, the book is useful as a readable tour of these technologies that helps explain why they so many people find them appealing.

# INDEX

Page numbers in **bold** font indicate the definition of a word used in a specific way for this book's purposes. Page numbers followed by "f" and "t" indicate figures and tables.

"it is a good use of my money," 29
"it is a good use of my time," 28–29
"it respects me," 29–30
"it takes me when I want to go," 28,
  159
"it takes me where I want to go,"
  26–28
overview of, 23–25, 27f
side issues and side effects and,
  25–26
Shifts, 73, 76, 80–82
Shopping center setbacks, 188–190
Shoup, Donald, 136
Side effects of transit, 25–26
Signal delays, 99, 101
Signal priority tools, 101
Simon Fraser University (British
  Columbia), 191f, 192
Simplicity, 31–32, 153–158
Singapore, 188, 189f
Slopes, stop spacing and, 63
Small-loop circulators, 57, 57f
Smartcards, 139–140, 141, 142, 144
Social-service objective, 118
Span of service, 28, 30, 85–86
Sparseville, **120–124**, 120f, 127–128,
  133–134, 220
Spatial Plan of 2004 (Canberra), 197,
  198f
Specialization, 49
Spectra, categories vs., 41–42
Speed
  concept of, 97
  delay and, 98
  freedom and, 31
  maps and, 89
  motorist's errors and, 41
  operating costs and, 33
  rapid vs. local service and, 70–71
  relative importance of, 2–3, 89
  travel time and, 29
Spiderweb grids, 170–172, 170f, 173f
Split shifts, 81
Spontaneity, requirement for, 31

S-shapes, 47, 53f
Stations, 26, 27f, 112–113. *See also*
  Stops
Stop spacing, 61–62, 63
Stops
  coverage of, 59–64, 60f, 62f, 63f,
    102
  density measurement and, 112–113
  express, rapid, and local, 64–66, 65f
  importance of location of, 26, 27f
  shift towards rapid, 66–71
Strategic Pubic Transport Network Plan
  (Canberra, Australia), 92–93
Subsidies, 13–14, 135–137
Suburbs, new, 192–196, 194f
Surrey, Canada, 178–179, 179f
Sustainability
  feedback loops and, 133–134
  rapid vs. local service and, 70–71
  residential density and, 111, 112
  transit lanes and, 106
Switzerland, 164
Sydney, Australia, 54, 139, 153–156,
  154f, 158, 160, 220
Syntagma Square (Athens), 178

Taxis, 14
Technology, as tool vs. goal, 6–7,
  216–217, 226
Telecommunications, 20
Terminology, 8, 44–46
Thatcher, Margaret, 42
Time of travel, 28–29, 141
Timing, connections and, 163
TOD. *See* Transit-Oriented
  Development
Tolls, 135
Tourism, 58
To/via problem, 54
Traffic delays, 99, 101, 167
Trains. *See* Rail transit
Transfer slips, 142
Transfers, 153
Transit, defined, **13–15**